fLANN O'bRIEN

AN ILLUSTRATED BIOGRAPHY

fLANN O'bRIEN

AN ILLUSTRATED BIOGRAPHY

❖

pETER COSTELLO
pETER VAN DE KAMP

BLOOMSBURY

First published in 1987 by
Bloomsbury Publishing Ltd., 2 Soho Square, London W1V 5DE

Copyright © 1987 by Peter Costello and Peter van de Kamp

Planned and produced by
Ryan Publishing Co. Ltd., Cardigan House, Union Road, Cambridge CB2 1HE

British Library Cataloguing in Publication Data

Costello, Peter
   Flann O'Brien: an illustrated biography.
   1. O'Brien, Flann 2. Authors, Irish—Biography
   I. Title II. Van de Kamp, Peter
   828'. 91409 PR6029.N56Z

   ISBN 0-7475-0129-7

The acknowledgement of copyright in pages 150-154
constitutes an extension of the copyright page.

Designed by Jole Bortoli
Typeset by Jamesway Graphics, Middleton, Manchester
Printed and Bound in Great Britain by WBC Print Ltd.

De Selby likens the position of a human on earth to that of a man on a tight-wire who must continue along the wire or perish, being, however free in all other respects. Movement in this restricted orbit results in the permanent hallucination known conventionally as 'life' with its innumerable concomitant limitations, afflictions and anomalies.

Flann O'Brien: *The Third Policeman*

Ne me demandez pas ce que j'aime et ce que je crois, n'allez pas au fond de mon âme.

Sainte-Beuve

CONTENTS

"Say, was that three fellahs? Or one fellah with three beards?"

Groucho Marx in
A Night at the Opera

INTRODUCTION

To many admirers of the novels of Flann O'Brien and the brilliant journalism of Myles na Gopaleen, the real man Brian O'Nolan is something of a mystery. He delighted in hiding his real personality behind a host of pen-names, of which those are only the best known. Under another pen-name, Stephen Blakesley, he was literally a man of mysteries, authoring a series of pulp detective thrillers. Discovering the facts about the real Brian O'Nolan has been for us something of a detective story.

This book had its origins in an exhibition mounted in Dublin to mark the twentieth anniversary of Brian O'Nolan's death. Much of the pictorial material we collected had never been seen in public before, especially the material lent to us by Mrs O'Nolan and the O'Nolan family, and aroused great interest, even among those who had known O'Nolan well. To those pictures we have now added an account of his life, the first extended biography to be written.

In Dublin Brian O'Nolan and his misadventures have become the subject of many anecdotes, most of which must be untrue. We have preferred the sobriety of fact to the apocrypha of Flann and the pseudo-gospels of Myles. We have found that many of the accepted facts about O'Nolan were merely legend, and that many of the legends were actually fact. His wife for instance doubts that he wrote the Blakesley novels! His life is like his own books, with disparate openings, multiple levels, a recycling hellishness, and a hardness which rivalled anything he described in Corkadorky.

In this pioneering exploration we have been lucky in having a great deal of help from those who thought they knew Brian O'Nolan, whether as husband, brother, student, civil servant, drinker, journalist, dog-lover, or novelist. It is clear that some of them knew different people, and that Brian O Nuallain (as he called himself in the privacy of his own mind) was not quite the same person as Brian O'Nolan, or Myles, or Flann. For much of his life he kept himself to himself.

We are deeply grateful to these people for all their help, which is acknowledged elsewhere, but our special thanks are due to Mrs Evelyn O'Nolan, who bore patiently with us. She deserves the special gratitude of all her husband's readers.

Peter Costello
Peter van de Kamp

Dublin and Leiden
September, 1987

For
EVELYN O'NOLAN

A Dublin Character

The date was 16 June, 1954, and though it was only mid-morning, Brian O'Nolan was already drunk.

This day was the fiftieth anniversary of Mr Leopold Bloom's wanderings through Dublin, which James Joyce had immortalised in *Ulysses*.

To mark this occasion a small group of Dublin literati had gathered at the Sandycove home of Michael Scott, a well-known architect, just below the Martello tower in which the opening scene of Joyce's novel is set. They planned to travel round the city through the day, visiting in turn the scenes of the novel, ending at night in what had once been the brothel quarter of the city, the area which Joyce had called Nighttown.

Sadly, no-one expected O'Nolan to be sober. By reputation, if not by sight, everyone in Dublin knew Brian O'Nolan, otherwise Myles na Gopaleen, the writer of the *Cruiskeen Lawn* column in the *Irish Times*. A few knew that under the name of Flann O'Brien, he had written in his youth a now nearly forgotten novel, *At Swim-Two-Birds*. Seeing him about the city, many must have wondered how a man with such extreme drinking habits, even for the city of Dublin, could have sustained a career as a writer.

As was his custom, he had been drinking that morning in the pubs around the Cattle Market, where customers, supposedly about their lawful business, would be served from 7.30 in the morning. Now retired from the Civil Service, on grounds of "ill-health", he was earning his living as a free-lance journalist, writing not only for the *Irish Times*, but for other papers and magazines under several pen-names. He needed to write for money as his pension was a tiny one. But this left little time for more creative work. In fact, O'Nolan no longer felt the urge to write other novels.

He had given them up as a "bad job". There was no money in that game, he would explain.

It was an old story in Dublin, which many other silenced writers in the city pubs could tell. O'Nolan's drinking was a release from the immense pressure under which he worked and lived. By now his dependence on alchohol was complete.

The rest of the party, that first Bloomsday, was made up of the poet Patrick Kavanagh, the young critic Anthony Cronin, a dentist named Tom Joyce, who as Joyce's cousin represented the family interest, and John Ryan, the painter and businessman who owned and edited the literary magazine *Envoy*. The idea of the Bloomsday celebration had been Ryan's, growing naturally out of a special Joyce issue of his magazine, for which O'Nolan had been guest editor.

Ryan had engaged two horse drawn cabs, of the old fashioned kind, which in *Ulysses* Mr Bloom and his friends drive to poor Paddy Dignam's funeral. The party were assigned roles from the novel. Cronin stood in for Stephen Dedalus, O'Nolan for his father Simon Dedalus, John Ryan for the journalist Martin Cunningham, and A. J. Leventhal, the Registrar of Trinity College, being Jewish, was recruited to fill (unknown to himself according to John Ryan) the role of Leopold Bloom.

"Was Joyce mad?" O'Nolan had asked in his editorial in *Envoy*. There was little doubt among Dubliners who encountered them that whatever about Joyce, this crowd were indeed mad.

O'Nolan, in the low Dublin accent he affected, had called the outing "the Jant"; his friend and former superior in the Civil Service, John Garvin, would later call it "a pilgrimace", partaking as it did of a pilgrimage, a grimace, and a disgrace.

Kavanagh and O'Nolan began the day by

J-DAY

THIS IS A SMALL, shy and simple article. It can be written only within the week or so in which a number of courageous men made off with about 200 rifles and a lesser amount of other lethal gear.

Every man concerned could have been shot dead. Why did they risk so much for so little?

* * *

THIS SHEER impulse to rebel, without regard to reason or results, is likely to be publicly commemorated this day. It is June 16th —and James Joyce wrote half a million words about what happened in Dublin on June 16th, 1904. The book is called "Ulysses" and is really the record of what happened a bona-fide traveller of that day,

CRUISKEEN LAWN
By
MYLES NA GOPALEEN

with, impaled in the text, an enormity of "philosophical material."

In this task Joyce did not go into somebody's workshop and choose the tools he needed: he took the whole lot. Thus does one find side by side monasticism and brothelism. St. Augustine himself perceived and recorded the "polarity" of virtue and vice, how one is integrally part of the other, and cannot exist without it. But not until James Joyce came along has anybody so considerably evoked depravity to establish the unextinguishable goodness of what is good.

* * *

I DO NOT WISH to provoke still another world war by invading America's monopoly of comment on the value of Joyce's work. People who insist that there is a junction of Cuffe street and Grafton street are, clearly, persons with whom not to argue. But I think I will risk a few remarks about Joyce, on the understanding that criticism without censure is intended.

Joyce was in no way what he is internationally acclaimed to be—a Dubliner. In fact there has been no more spectacular non-Dubliner. Not once did he tire of saying that he was never at home. This absence may have been a necessity of his literary method, but it has often

occurred to my irreverent self that maybe he hadn't the fare.

Joyce was a bad writer. He was too skilled in some departments of writing, and could not resist the *tour de force*. Parts of "Ulysses" are of unreadable boredom. One thinks of a violinist corrupting with "cadenza" a work wherein the composing master had in the text practised masterly abstention from fireworks. Beethoven had a big row with the violinist Kreutzer on this very point.

Joyce was illiterate. He had a fabulously developed jackdaw talent of picking up bits and pieces, but it seems his net was too wide to justify getting a few kids' schoolbooks and learning the rudiments of a new language correctly. Every foreign-language quotation in any of his works known to me are wrong. His few sallies at Greek are wrong, and his few attempts at a Gaelic phrase are absolutely monstrous. Anybody could have told him the right thing. Why did he not bother to ask?

* * *

THAT LAST QUESTION evokes a complementary question, of which there is no mention on the horizonless hog of American exegesis. Was the man a leg-puller? Was "Finnegans Wake" the ultimate fantasy in cod? Did he seek to evolve for himself, chiefly by talking in strict confidence to stooges, mostly American, a mythical personality? Did . . . (*pardon me while I swallow this yellow capsule!*) . . . did . . . James Joyce ever exist?

* * *

IT SEEMS he did, and that he done what he done. There is something intimidatingly authentic about print. My own first contact with the man in a literary collision was a quotation fired at me. This: "I go to encounter for the millionth time the reality of experience and to forge in the smithy of my soul the uncreated conscience of my race."

Many a time had I read that piece with admiration. In recent years I have asked a few wise men what the words mean. They mean nothing.

But are they intended to mean nothing, in the sense of meaning something exact? Or are they intended to suggest an imponderable theme for reflection, as night—day— life—death—are used in various patterns in "Finnegans Wake?"

* * *

JOYCE'S MAIN WORK, "Ulysses," is "not banned" in Ireland, which means simply that any person asking for it in a bookshop would probably be lynched. Parts of it are pornographic, though the motive appears to have been of the best; Bernard Shaw acknowledged the purity of Joyce's mind, and his skill and courage in presenting a portrait of *fin de siècle* brutality and horrors are evident in a letter which Miss Patricia Hutchins quotes in her interesting book, "James Joyce's Dublin." I ask— though no Bowdler I — is it not a great pity that an expurgated edition of "Ulysses" is not published, *virginibus puerisque?*

It would surely establish the utterly ignored fact that Joyce was among the most comic writers who have ever lived. Every time I get influenza I read about The Citizen and his Dog; penicillin has nothing on them.

* * *

IT IS NOT EASY to close up satisfactorily this unpremeditated note. A number of ideas come to the surface.

Here is one. Would it appear blanshardish for a committee of reputable Dublin citizens, in Mansion House assembled, to petition the Holy Father to do what a distinguished predecessor did, and suppress the Jesuit Order, and turn Clongowes Wood College into something else?

Who can be answerable for James Joyce if it be not the Jesuits?

Brian O'Nolan in the early 1950s (*facing previous page*).

Cruiskeen Lawn article written for the first Bloomsday (*this page*). The incidents of Bloomsday, as drawn by John Ryan for *Envoy* special issue on Joyce (*opposite*).

BLOOMSDAY

16th June, 1904

Myles with Anthony Cronin, from John Ryan's film of the first Bloomsday *(top)*. **Cronin urges in the novelist** *(middle)*. **Myles poor mouthing** *(bottom)*.

Myles leaves the beach, relieved *(top).*
Myles suspects the camera *(middle).*
**Myles and Con Leventhal await their cab
on Strand Road** *(bottom).*

Pause for refreshment in Irishtown —
John Ryan with Tom Joyce and curious
Dubliners *(top)*. A bewildered Myles in
the middle of things *(middle)*. Myles and
Patrick Kavanagh — who later died of
lung cancer *(bottom)*.

deciding they must climb up to the Martello tower itself, which stood on a granite shoulder behind the house. As Cronin recalls, Kavanagh hoisted himself up the steep slope above O'Nolan, who snarled in anger and laid hold of his ankle. Kavanagh roared, and lashed out with his foot. Fearful that O'Nolan would be kicked in the face by the poet's enormous farmer's boot, the others hastened to rescue and restrain the rivals.

With some difficulty O'Nolan was stuffed into one of the cabs by Cronin and the others. Then they were off, along the seafront of Dublin Bay, and into the city.

In pubs along the way an enormous amount of alcohol was consumed, so much so that on Sandymount Strand they had to relieve themselves as Stephen Dedalus does in *Ulysses*. Tom Joyce and Cronin sang the sentimental songs of Thomas Moore which Joyce had loved, such as *Silent O Moyle* and *A Pale Moon was Shining*. O'Nolan recounted a long and incoherent tale of misadventure in the Irish Club in London. They stopped in Irishtown to listen to the running of the Ascot Gold Cup on a radio in a betting shop, but eventually they arrived in Duke Street in the city centre, and the Bailey, which John Ryan then ran as a literary pub.

They went no further. Once there another drink seemed more attractive than a long tour of Joycean slums, and the siren call of the long vanished pleasures of Nighttown.

The day had been a light-hearted spree, a mere "jant" indeed, typical of the antics of Bohemian Dublin in the 1950's. The brooding influences of Yeats and Joyce was passing away with their deaths. A newer, livelier spirit was in the air, soon to find expression in the ribaldries of J. P. Donleavy's novel *The Ginger Man*, the verbal fireworks of Brendan Behan's plays, and the irreverent criticism of Anthony Cronin.

But in this decade Brian O'Nolan and his friend Paddy Kavanagh were odd men out, publishing no books of their own. Their first books had appeared just before the war, and though they were highly praised, through unfortunate circumstances went out of circulation very quickly. Enemy bombing destroyed O'Nolan's novel in his London publisher's warehouse, Kavanagh's book was suppressed following a libel action. Now both earned their way by writing newspaper columns (Kavanagh had even been a film critic), nursing as best they could the real talents which the world

around them seemed to value so little. They had become professional journalists, amateur artists.

O'Nolan, in his old brown hat and crumpled overcoat, was a familiar figure to Dubliners in what was still a small tightly-knit city. Like Kavanagh he had become for the public that almost sinister thing, a Dublin character.

A shy man, O'Nolan abhorred this. To many he could be extremely rude. He preferred to drink alone, elbows on the bar to ward off social intercourse. From the deep bitterness of artistic frustration, he seemed to be seeking a permanent solace in drink. Every contemporary of his claims to have had an encounter with the foul-mouthed Myles.

Yet this was only a superficial, public idea of the man. If he started drinking early, he was always home by four. O'Nolan was the one man in the city who hardly ever saw closing time in a public house. Drunk or sober he had a passion for the printed word. He read, rather than talked, in pubs. In the Bailey that day he appears as he so often did with a book in his hand, while the rest of the party argue behind him.

He worked constantly, writing sometimes six columns a week. His copy was always ready for his editors, many thousands of words, all the result of hard work, constant observation and creative thought. The talents many now wished he had devoted to his novels, he poured into his articles.

Whatever his appearance in public, and the bitter rancour of the drinker which was all too often turned on friend and foe alike, O'Nolan contained within him a very different person. Sean O'Faolain, the victim of many sharp comments in *Cruiskeen Lawn*, recalls this real man as "genial, adult, sceptical, courteous and sympathetic to others."

A few years before O'Nolan had published a translation from a medieval Irish poem of a scribe complaining of the pain in his hand from the amount of writing he had to do.

My hand has a pain from writing,
Not steady the sharp tool of my craft,
Its slender beak spews bright ink—
A beetle-dark shining draught . . .

My little dribbly pen stretches
Across the great white paper plain,
Insatiable for splendid riches—
That is why my hand has pain!

The cabs approaching Sandymount Strand *(above)*.

The Bloomsday pilgrims on the beach: left to right — John Ryan, Anthony Cronin, Myles, Patrick Kavanagh, and Tom Joyce *(below)*.

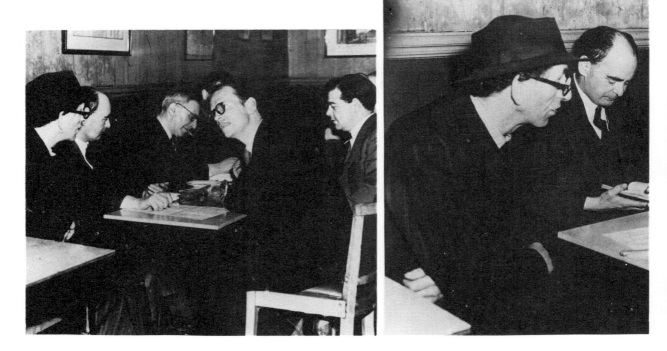

There was clearly a personal understanding in this poem, but his version compared with rival translators such as Frank O'Connor, who have won great praise, is hard, bright, and penetrating. It reveals the real quality of O'Nolan's mind.

From the Dublin character of the literary drunk, that real man emerged when he sat down to write.

During these years in the early 1950's, O'Nolan's column in the *Irish Times* took on a more satirical, a more engaged tone, with comments on the public life of the city and the country that struck home. He could hurt, but it gave him only temporary pleasure. He had made himself a brilliant journalist, but this did not fulfil his real creative needs. He never wished to have the pieces collected and published as a proper book — though he made an exception for his Keats and Chapman jokes.

The lesson of Joyce, whom O'Nolan and his friends had been celebrating that day, was always before him. Joyce had put everything in his life aside to finish his books. For him carrying out the original intention was an heroic effort. But O'Nolan had no time for such heroism. In 1954 there didn't seem to be another book in Brian O'Nolan.

He had always admired Joyce. What Irish writer does not? But he became dismayed as slowly through the 1950's he saw the emergence of a "Joyce Industry". O'Nolan's reputation fell as Joyce's rose to new heights — a reissue of *At Swim-Two-Birds* in New York in 1951 had been a resounding failure. He

Outside Davy Byrne's "moral pub", the end of the pilgrimage *(opposite top)*.

The pilgrims at rest — Joycean dialogue between Cronin, Kavanagh and Myles *(opposite bottom left)*.

Myles the bookhandler, oblivious now to the discourse of the poets *(opposite bottom right)*.

Aerial view of Dublin in the 1950s *(above)*.

81 Merrion Avenue
Blackrock,
Dublin,
Ireland.

24th May, 1950.

Dear Sir,

In reply to your letter of
the 16th regarding the proposed Joyce
Exhibition in London, I enclose a copy
of the book you mention. It is not mine,
and I would be glad to get it back in
due course.

In regard to letters from
Joyce, he asked me some years ago to
make some confidential inquiries on
business and family matters. Apart from
the fact that the letters are of no
literary interest whatever , I don't
think it would be proper to exhibit
them publicly.

Yours sincerely,

Brian O'Nolan

Ewan Phillips, Esq.,
Director,
The Institute of Contemporary Arts,
17-18 Dover Street,
Piccadilly,
London, W.1.

refused to release his own letters from Joyce, as he considered such documents to be private. Visiting American scholars were eager to follow the Bloomsday round that he had inaugurated, and he hated it.

Dublin folklore has it that O'Nolan and his cronies cashed in on the rising interest in Joyceana by selling these scholars old battered hats which had purportedly belonged to Joyce. To Richard Ellmann, Joyce's biographer, O'Nolan was merely "a Dublin journalist" who claimed to have hoaxed the academic world with a fake interview with Joyce's father, which Gorman and Ellmann had taken seriously. O'Nolan loved unsettling the complacent, but his claim was untrue, though loyal friends in Dublin still repeat it.

He knew his own achievement — whatever he might say about it to his friends — was also a considerable one. But his book, despite being reissued in America, was forgotten. No-one paid O'Nolan any attention.

But he had not lost all his followers. In 1960 an adventurous young publisher named Timothy O'Keefe persuaded his London firm, MacGibbon and Kee, to reissue *At Swim-Two-Birds*. Now at last the merits of that 1939 novel were recognised. It was received with the highest kinds of praise, though this was not always couched in a manner that pleased him ("A comic heir of James Joyce", exclaimed the London *Observer*). He had it seems outdone Joyce by inventing the anti-novel twenty years before its time, the magical-realistic novel forty years before its time.

At Swim-Two-Birds was soon issued in a mass-market paperback, and is now enshrined as a Penguin Modern Classic. The effect on O'Nolan was almost sobering. Once again he began to write something more than journalism. Quickly two more novels by "Flann O'Brien" were produced to the delight of his admirers. In *The Hard Life* he got his own back on Joyce, reducing him to sewing semmits for the Jesuits. Despite a serious breakdown in 1962, and periods of ill-health, O'Nolan was back on course.

For Brian O'Nolan at the age of fifty it was something like a new beginning, a fresh start in life.

James Joyce, whose life and work cast a shadow over O'Nolan's generation *(top)*.

Brian O'Nolan writes in 1950 about his correspondence with Joyce, letters now lost *(bottom)*.

The Absent Father

Brian O'Nolan's life, beset with mysteries and evasions, began on 5 October 1911 at 15 Bowling Green, Strabane, a small town in the northern county of Tyrone, 12 miles from Derry.

"Biography", O'Nolan once wrote, "is the lowest form of letters and is atrophied by the subject's own censorship, conscious or otherwise." His own childhood, however, is fairly well-documented from accounts by his brothers Ciaran and Kevin, and so beyond the subjects urge to confabulate his fortunes and failures.

Brian was the third child in a family of twelve, seven boys and five girls. His mother Agnes Gormley was the daughter of a John Gormley of Omagh, who had settled in Strabane soon after her birth in 1886. The Gormleys ran a shop in the High Street, dealing as such shops do in provincial Ireland in a little bit of everything. Her family were strongly involved in Irish cultural activities in the town — Brian's uncle was a noted musician. The family were educated people, but also colourful and outgoing in speech and manners. Brian's gift for language owes much to the eloquence of his mother's family.

His father was very much Agnes' counterpart. Where hers was a gentle, down-to-earth nature, with a love of song, his was a taciturn and disciplined intellect. Michael Victor Nolan (the style of O'Nolan was adopted by his children) was born near Omagh in 1875, and was a university graduate. By occupation he was a Customs and Excise Officer, collecting the tax revenue from local distilleries, of which there were over a hundred in the country at that time. He met his wife while stationed in Strabane, and they were married in Murlough church on 5 September 1906.

Under his intransigent exterior Michael Nolan harboured secret literary ambitions —

his brothers were writers, and one had a play produced at the Abbey in 1920. After his death the script of a detective novel was found among his papers. It had been well received by the reader at Collins before the Great War, but his agent advised him not to accept their offer as it was too low. (This incident was to have an echo in his son's troubles with *The Third Policeman*, which is also a murder story of sorts.)

The resemblance of Michael Nolan's graduation photograph to Brian's is almost uncanny, and overall father and son seem to have had much in common. Like his father, Brian concealed his real self from the world.

The peculiar nature of his job compelled Michael Nolan to move about the country. Soon after Brian was born the family moved to Glasgow, to the suburb of Uddington. From there they moved to Inchicore, outside Dublin, where they were living at the time of the Easter Rising in 1916 and felt the shock of the rebellion.

Early in 1917 Michael Nolan was promoted to the rank of Surveyor, which involved even more travel. He moved the family back to Strabane to be near their relatives while he toured the country on his professional duties. He rented a house in Ballycolman Lane, which, according to Kevin O'Nolan, was haunted. Agnes Gormley and her family were, by his account, somewhat psychic, and she took the noises at night, the odd rumblings and the banging of shutters in her stride. Her husband did not, and brought his brother up to bless the house. There must have been an odd atmosphere in that home. As a disturber of the peace that poltergeist has something in common with the mischievous spirit of Myles na Gopaleen.

In 1920 the family moved again, this time to near Tullamore, in the midland county of

Strabane — the Mourne Bridge and river in O'Nolan's youth *(top)*.

O'Nolan's mother as a young woman *(bottom left)*.

O'Nolan's father in his graduation robes *(bottom right)*.

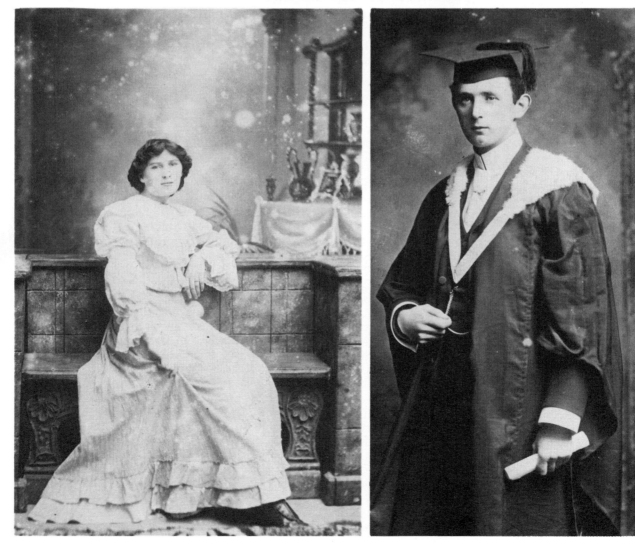

Ballycolman Lane, Strabane, scene of childhood years *(top left).*

Brian with family *(top right).*

The O'Nolan children outside the house at Cappincur *(bottom).*

Offaly, where Michael was now stationed. They lived in a large house called The Beeches, at Cappincur, two miles outside the town. Nearby was the famous distillery, Locke's of Kilbeggan, from which Mr Collopy gets his jar of whiskey in *The Hard Life*, O'Nolan's later novel.

Little as yet had been done to school the children. Their father on his travels would occasionally set them written exercises, but mostly the children more or less educated themselves — with great success, judging from their future careers. At home Irish was the common language. Their father seems to have discouraged them from playing with other children for fear they would speak English. A younger brother, Michael, recalls how they learnt their English from comics borrowed from their Gormley cousins, who had easy access to such forbidden fare in the family shop.

Irish, then, was their mother, or rather, father tongue. Their uncle, the Rev. Gearoid O Nuallain (he used the Irish form of the name) was a famous Irish scholar, and Professor of Irish at Maynooth — the college which trains many of the priests of Ireland. The reverend professor was a sociable man, with a penchant for colourful, if slightly unclerical language. He had taken over the professorship after the dismissal of Dr O'Hickey, a hero of the playwright Sean O'Casey, who had fallen out with the Hierarchy over the question of compulsory Irish in the National University of Ireland. Some Nationalist and Irish language enthusiasts regarded Fr O Nuallain askance. Brian, in his turn, was to treat them with scornful suspicion in later life.

Life at The Beeches was close to idyllic, an outdoor life in gardens and fields, with a canal nearby for fishing and swimming, and pleasant, hospitable neighbours in the Daly family, and the occasional visitor. For twenty years after they left the house the butcher in Kilbeggan used to send a joint of beef up to Mrs Nolan in Dublin for the family Sunday lunch. But even here the outside world impinged, for the road outside the house was travelled during the Troubles by British patrols. Michael Nolan took care that his children, with their patriotic sentiments, did not come in contact with them.

New arrangements after the creation of the Irish Free State brought Michael Nolan up to Dublin in 1925 to work in the Revenue Commissioners offices in Dublin Castle. He

Brian with his sister *(opposite top).*

Brian with his brother — a hint of things to come *(opposite bottom).*

The solemn Brian with his brothers and sisters, aged 8 *(this page).*

took a house in the city centre, 25 Herbert Place, alongside the tree-lined Grand Canal, of whose "leafy-with-love" banks Patrick Kavanagh was to write in his famous *"Canal Bank Walk"*. Here the barges could still be seen sailing by for the Midlands. *The Hard Life* is set in a house on the next terrace along the canal, Wilton Place; but Kevin O'Nolan believes that details of the house in the novel were supplied by Brian's childhood home.

Life now changed. The parents were frequent theatre goers, and the house filled up with old programmes leafed through with fascination by the children. They were now old enough to be left to their own devices. The top floor of the five-storey Georgian house was given over to playrooms. Brian's brothers had laid down a toy railway track—beginning for Brian that fascination with trains so evident in *Cruiskeen Lawn*, and in the notorious essay on Joyce, *"A Bash in the Tunnel"*. Brian's

creativity at this time was focused on the visual. He was an excellent draftsman, and a large amount of his energy went into the creation of what the children called "films", cartoon strips which they illustrated for themselves, and wrote storylines for. He also took up photography and processed his pictures in his own dark room. But occasionally his photographic chemicals served for boyish pranks: at night passers-by were startled by a ghostly glare of flashlight powder from a top-floor window-sill. The eerie phenomenon stopped when the police seemed to interest themselves in the matter.

The children also transformed the house into a theatre, but family plays, family directed and with a family cast, were not always polished enough to please parents who enjoyed professional drama. Brian was by now an accomplished violinist, and musical evenings at least pleased the performers.

It was at this time in the early 1920's that the children had at last to comply with the demands of a more formal and disciplined education. Brian and his brothers were thrown in at the deep end; they were sent to the Christian Brothers' school in Synge Street, renowned for its rigidly basic and brutally applied methods of education. Brian seems to have been grateful for the thorough grounding he got here in languages, though in his *Cruiskeen Lawn* columns and in *The Hard Life* the school is mentioned with utter disdain.

In 1927 the family moved again, to 4 Avoca Terrace in the sea-side suburb of Blackrock. This house would prove to be the final family home. The house was spacious enough to hold the large family. Brian was to live there for over twenty years, and to write his earliest, and perhaps his finest books. Michael Nolan was now a Revenue Commissioner. The boys were sent (as befitted this new status) to Blackrock College, a prestigious school more famous for rugby than scholarship, where de Valera, soon to be the country's leading politician, had been both a student and

Michael Victor Nolan in middle age *(opposite top left)*.

Herbert Place, Dublin, on the Grand Canal *(opposite top right)*.

Brian's mother in later years *(opposite bottom)*.

Brian O'Nolan aged 12 *(top)*.

The literary uncle, Fr Gearoid O Nuallain *(bottom)*.

teacher.

Like many dear personal memories, Blackrock College is completely absent from O'Nolan's writings. Throughout his life he had links with the school: its priests attended him in the last months of his life and went to his funeral.

Despite the unorthodox nature of their education, the O'Nolan boys carried away the school prizes during the years they attended Blackrock. A photograph of 1928 shows Brian among a group of prize winners, near Vivion de Valera, the son of the great man. This was not a context that was to reappear in later life.

The school may also have refined his literary style. An *Irish Times* colleague, Bruce Williamson, says that in the 1940's two prose styles were admired in Dublin: the satirical columns of Flann O'Brien and the pastorals of Dr John Charles McQuaid, by then Archbishop of Dublin (due it was rumoured at the time, to the influence of his friend Mr de Valera). Brian O'Nolan's entry papers for his matriculation exams bear the witnessing signature of McQuaid, then Dean of Studies at Blackrock College. As editor of the college

MAIN STREET, STRABANE.

Main Street, Strabane, with the cousins' shop on right *(top).*

4 Avoca Terrace, where *At Swim-Two-Birds* was written *(bottom).*

Student group at Blackrock College, 1928. Brian O'Nolan *(top left)* **with Vivion de Valera on right** *(opposite top).*

O'Nolan's writing, in imitation of Dr McQuaid's, from a schoolbook *(opposite bottom).*

annual Dr McQuaid published O'Nolan's literary creation, a Shakespearean lyric entitled "Ad Astra":

> Ah! when the skies at night
>   Are damascened with gold,
> Methinks the endless sight
>   Eternity unrolled.

More curiously at the back of Brian's copy of Thomas a Kempis in Irish, Brian has imitated Dr McQuaid's handwriting, including an excuse from all work. This is the earliest known parody of style from his fluent pen.

Brian left his mark on the school with the first of a long line of indignant cries against the establishment. He led a campaign to resist the wearing of the school blazers which were then made in England. On a wall visible from the road he painted the slogan, "Burn British Blazers", a cryptic messsage which must have puzzled passers by.

It may be significant, in looking back over these early years, that in O'Nolan's novels there are no identifiable parents, only uncles and brothers, and that in *At Swim-Two-Birds* the created character is intent upon destroying its creator. Perhaps a father absent from his real world has been erased completely from his fictional universe. Or perhaps Brian was too close to his father to put him into his fiction. His brother Ciaran relates that when he was working on his own first novel, in the same room as his father sat in the evenings, Michael Nolan never inquired about what he was doing. There was he says "a communication gap". Kevin O'Nolan says the children took themselves off to college as it pleased them to do, and their father might not even have known they were going there.

His civil servant father, his academic uncle, in his own family Brian had models for several careers. From adolescence, he seems to have searched for a guardian to give shape to his life.

Scholaireachtai.   Euclid elements

Greek   Sgrudughadh intinne.

Scholarchip.   Sgrudughadh intinne.
                                                              Please.
                        Ca bhfhuair tu é.   excuse
                                                              for all
Imitatio Christi.   Imitatio Christi   work

   Imitatio Christi   Aithris an Chriost.

To interest, to amuse to elevate.

   Avoca Terrace Blackrock College. Williamstown

Matriculation.

Before filling in particulars below, see page 4.   3   1187

1. Surname [see note 7 at foot of page 2.] . . .	Ó Nualláin
2. Christian Names in full, ...	Brian
3. Date and Place of Birth, with nature of accompanying evidence of age. If you have previously entered for this examination, no further *evidence* of age will be required; but the exact date of birth must be stated opposite.	Date 5th October 1911. Certified Extract from Register of Births Place Bowling Green, Strabane.
4. Name, Residence, and Occupation of Father. Even in the case of a Father being deceased, his name and late occupation must be given.	Michael O Nualláin. 4 Avoca Terrace Blackrock Revenue Commissioner
5. If you have previously entered for this examination, state the date, or dates.	—
6. Details of fee enclosed, whether it be P.O. Order, Bank Note, etc.	Cheque. £-
7. School or Schools in which you were educated during the past twelve months.	Blackrock College Dublin
8. If a Student of any College or of any other University, state the fact, and date of Matriculation. N.B.—Students of Colleges or of any other University must forward herewith a Certificate showing date of Matriculation and present standing therein.	620
9. Here state the subjects in which you intend to present yourself for Examination. † Not more than five subjects may be selected. N.B.—The selection of these subjects must be strictly in accordance with the regulations as to groups set forth in detail in the Regulations and Courses for the Matriculation Examination.	N.B.—Candidates will be examined *only* in the subjects here stated. 1 Irish. 2 English. 3 Mathematics. 4 Latin. 5 History.
10.*(a) Here state the subject or subjects, if any, from which you claim exemption at this examination, on the grounds of having passed in these subjects, at the Matriculation Examination in or after 1928, or at an outside examination recognised for this purpose by the University. (See Regulations and Courses for the Matriculation Examination.) (b) Here state the Examination on account of which you claim exemption from the above subject or subjects, and the date of the Examination. (*In the case of Senior Grade Examination, or Leaving Certificate Examination, state also your number at that Examination.*)	PASSED Examination — Date — Examination Number —
11. Usual residence, that is home address.	4 Avoca Terrace Blackrock
Centre, taken from list on page 2, at which you wish to be examined.	Dublin

DECLARATION.

I......Brian Ó Nualláin......hereby declare that if I pass the Matriculation Examination I will observe and obey the Statutes and Regulations of the National University of Ireland as far as they concern me, and pay due respect and obedience to the Chancellor and other officers of the University, and I further declare that *the entire of the above Form has been filled up in my handwriting.*

Candidate's usual Signature......Brian Ua Nualláin

Address to which communications up to the time of the Examination are to be addressed } ......Blackrock College Dublin

Dated....24th....day of....April....1929

† Engineering Students, if they so desire, may present six subjects to fulfil requirements of Institution of Civil Engineers
* The Certificate of having passed an outside Examination, in respect of which exemption is claimed, must be lodged as evidence with this Form

[SEE PAGE 4

CERTIFICATE OF WITNESS.

[To be completed by Magistrate, Clergyman, or Head of School attended by Candidate.

I certify that this form of entry has been filled up in my presence by

B. O Nuallain

Candidate for the Matriculation Examination, and that I know the said Candidate.

Signature, ... J m'Quaid. 63.54

Address, ... Blackrock College.
...... Dublin.

Description (*i.e.*, Magistrate, Clergyman, or Head of School attended by Candidate) ...... Dean of Studies

Application for UCD filled out by Brian O'Nolan . . .(*top left*).

. . . and signed by Dr McQuaid (*top right*).

The key figure in these years was another uncle, Joe Gormley, who worked as a journalist and entertaining sports writer with a special interest in greyhound racing. Brian soon shared his enthusiasm: an article he wrote for *The Bell*, the literary magazine of the 1940's, dealt with the history and arcana of "going to the dogs". Through his uncle's connections, Brian had access to the Dublin newspaper world.

Brian was clearly a person of distinction: his intent, withdrawn face gazes out of the family photos, revealing him as a person of character, even as a child. Yet O'Nolan's literary genius was not yet apparent. At this time it was his elder brother Ciaran who was the literary light of the family. With the help of Brian, he ran a family newspaper called *The Observer*. Ciaran, not Brian, was the one who scribbled "novels" into penny notebooks.

From his childhood Brian carried away little of literary value. The fields around Cappincur, the flat boggy brownness of the midlands, may have contributed something to the setting of *The Third Policeman*. And surely the policemen themselves in that novel are the Royal Irish Constabulary of the British era rather than the Civil Guards of the Irish Free State? But of Strabane and the Ulster family connections, there is almost nothing, beyond a few anecdotes in his columns. To the end of his life Brian loved the town and that part of the world. But as a writer it gave him very little. Dublin, where he was an outsider, gave him more, but only what echoed an already familiar literary shape in the writings of Joyce.

Undoubtedly O'Nolan loved the scenes of his childhood, the memories of his parents, the adventures with his brothers and sisters. But life in rural Ireland and in provincial towns, that kind of stuff was the material of Frank O'Connor and Sean O'Faolain, Francis Mac-Manus and Benedict Kiely. It held nothing of value to Brian O'Nolan. He didn't want to make a literature of life, but a literature of literature.

St Stephen's Green in the 1930s — the Boer War Memorial and the Shelbourne Hotel *(above)*.

University College, Earlsfort Terrace, setting for *At Swim-Two-Birds* *(opposite)*

College Years

Brian O'Nolan entered University College, Dublin, in October 1929 —"the second day of Michaelmas Term" to be exact. The college was then in the old Royal University buildings in Earlsfort Terrace in the city centre. A modern facade concealed what at the rear was semiruinous. There, and nearby in No. 86 St Stephen's Green (the university building described in Joyce's *Portrait of the Artist*), he began to live a new life as a celebrated character.

At first he was quiet and unobtrusive, a student who obtained satisfactory but unstartling results in his First Year course: a pass in Latin, English, German and Logic, and second class honours in Irish.

It was only during his second year (1930/31) that he emerged as a college personality, though not through any of the more formal college clubs and groups, but as a gadfly speaker in the college debating society, the Literary and Historical Society, and L and H.

The student body then numbered only 1,931, small perhaps by today's standards, but they included (as visitors to the L and H were often reminded), the future leaders of the nation. Even among this selfregarding elite, this potential national establishment, O'Nolan stood out.

A contemporary, P. F. O'Donovan, later recalled: "None of us will forget the debating genius of Brian O'Nolan who was the best impromptu speaker the Society knew in those days, because from the first all his speeches were impromptu and likely to contain a sharp barb even for the unwary chairman attempting to bring him to order." The lineaments of the future daily columnist, an impromptu stylist if ever there was one, are readily discernible here.

Aside from the formal inaugural, the L and H met on Saturday nights in the Old Physics Theatre in No. 86. A huge crowd, often including outsiders, would attend. Only a fraction of them could get into the room. The rest stayed outside on the landing, baying and

University College, Newman House, where Joyce had studied *(top)*.

Cartoon by Brian O'Nolan, perhaps recalling the blatherers at the L and H *(bottom)*.

The interior of John Hartigan's pub in Lower Leeson Street, a haunt of UCD students *(opposite)*.

ⱅⱅⱅⱅ AN FIR ÓLⱅA

bⱤIAN UA NUALLÁIN DO CEAP

bawling at the speakers inside. O'Nolan was the darling of "the Mob", and for three years he was recognised as the leader of this informal opposition. It was a role that he delighted in.

It is recalled that when the death of a notorious Hollywood actress was announced, O'Nolan observed to the Mob that she was now "screwed inside her coffin". On another memorable occasion O'Nolan had to speak without preparation on the theme of "Sweet are the uses of advertisement", which he did using as his text an ad in his evening newspaper with the headline: "I wonder does he see that faded slip". What began in a frivolous mood slowly, and for many in the audience surprisingly, turned towards the end into something far more thoughtful, on the dangerous manipulations of the press in the modern day.

But O'Nolan found himself typecast as the college funny man, and it was a role he could not easily escape. When in the session 1932/33 he decided to run for Auditor against Vivion de Valera, the son of the prime minister, he was defeated 42 votes to 12. He had stated that he did not care for the dominant role which the politically inspired played in the affairs of the L and H. This was a futile protest: for the society was a serious proving-ground for future barristers, ministers, judges and presidents.

In 1932 O'Nolan was awarded the society's Impromtu Medal, one of five in the gift of the society. (As with so many points in O'Nolan's career, there is some confusion about this medal. O'Nolan says he "amassed some medals"; but the College Calendar states that he won the first year medal in his second year, while the records of the L and H say he won only the Impromtu.) The gold and silver medals were won by the formal speakers — one of them by a future High Court Judge and President of Ireland, Carrol O'Daly. The award did not mean that O'Nolan was the best speaker in the society, but that he was one of the most effective and colourful.

The open debate, however, was not the only forum in which he flourished. In May 1931 the Students Representative Council revamped

Scéala Éireann, 2/1/1932

the college paper under a new title *Com-hthrom Feinne* (the motto of UCD). O'Nolan became a frequent contributor, and actual editor for a period. Here he could give his comic genius full range, under the pen-name of Brother Barnabus, the first of a long series of literary personas.

Poems, stories and articles by others paled beside his comic inventions which became increasingly outrageous. The long-suffering college porters were featured continuously in the parts of Mutt and Jeff, de Valera and Douglas Hyde (the professor of Irish in UCD), Hitler and Mussolini. In the character of Lionel Prune the poet W.B. Yeats was mercilessly caricatured, not in the full vigour of his maturity but as the willowy creature of the Celtic Twilight. A serious side to O'No-lan's nature appeared in an article about the

executed patriot who had been a student at UCD, Kevin Barry; and another later article about the future of the L and H itself.

But in the eyes of his admirers O'Nolan was not allowed to exit from the burlesque stage on which they wished to share for as long as they could. He all too often reflected their own prejudices. His remarks on the college girls had, so *Comhthrom Feinne* claimed, to be censored, but the full text could be read on application. The modesty of the young ladies associated with the Pro-Fide group (a religious society concerned with Catholic social action which was politically inclined to the right) especially aroused the ribaldry of the male students. O'Nolan's known aversion to women led to his name being coupled by the paper with one of the more reserved of the college girls, a certain Mary Wyer, who was studying commerce:

> The alluring and coy M-lly W-r,
> As she swam in the Mull of Cantrye,
> Remarked to the fishes,
> "I've got all my wishes,
> It's Brine Oh! No land I desire."

Brother Barnabus, whose ascetic puritanism reflected O'Nolan's own character very well, yet seems to have spent much of his time recuperating in such German watering places as Baden-Baden, predicted in his college almanac for 1932 that Brian O'Nolan and his friends would gain first class honours and a travelling studentship. Such would be the shock that reviving brandy would be called for.

In the event O'Nolan passed his Honours degree with a pass in German, and a second class pass in Irish and English. This was not quite the "brilliant" result recalled by college legend. But it must be recalled that O'Nolan was now contributing at this time stories and articles in Irish to the *Irish Press* and to its sister paper *The Evening Press*. O'Nolan began his career as a journalist while he was still at university, long before the appearance of Myles na Gopaleen.

At college O'Nolan gave the impression that he hardly worked at all. He played billiards and cards, and in the pub in Lower Leeson Street frequented by students, Grogan's, laid the foundation of his drinking habits. He claimed that the education provided was an indifferent one, and he delighted in successful-

í Maireann an Sóg act Seal

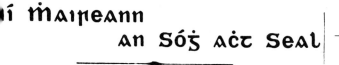

Slioct de Stair Fáisteanaig

'ra bliain 2058 A.D. a cuireað cup ap an ueag-obaiṗ i scéas-uaiṗ. ṫpacaið na bliana ṗin, cáinic taoḋ ḋip tiomċa lán-ċiallṁaṗ uaḋ, ann aboat Gogarty ó'n Oilceán Úp aṗ ṗṗo cuiṁ Éipinn aguṗ cá a ṫompáð aṁ aiṗ-ṗin ṗuṗ eiṗeann a ḃuail an b coiṗcéim aṗ ḃealaḟ an Cṗa Nua. An ueag-feaṗ ṗeo ag ṗṗaiṗceoṗaḋ ṫapa aṗ ċṗaċonṗ an 23aṫ Meiṫeaṁ i cataṗ i nDún Laoġaiṗe aguṗ ḃí ċaṗa ṗeo aṗ iṁ iṗe go ṫeoṗ ṗéaḋtaḟ ṗṁeaċa ṗán aṁḋpoṁ ḃuaiḋeaṗta ṗṗaċṁaṗ a ḃ'ṗulaing Éiṗe ṗaoi act Sapana aṁiaṗ aṗ ṙaṗa aoiṗ ḃe cuṗo aṗ ṁTiġeaṗna, aguṗ ḃí e ṁóṗa ionṗancaiṗ ag ṗcoilceaḋ ḋin an coiṁiṗceiṗe i n-agaiḋ an uiaiṗce. Ḃpiṗeaḋ a cuṁo ṗoiġne aṁ ḃeiṗeaḋ, aguṗ cáinic ṗioṗṗaḋ ṁce uaṗú:

" England ! " aṗ ṗeiṗean. " And ṫ the heck didn't you buy the ṗṗ years ago ? "*

Anoiṗ, cé ḃeaḋ 'ṗa caṗa ṗeo act aḋaṗ ṫeann, uuine oilḃeaṗic móṗ ṗṫaṁ ḃe cuṗo na h-Éipeann. Ḃí Lán-léiġeanta ḃeaḋ-oilce aguṗ ṁ niṁe aiṗe i ṗceannc ċiallṁaṗ. ṗcníṗ ṗé go ṗaḋ ṗcoil na céille cainnc ṗeo. Le h-iṁ ċeaṗc an aṁa, aiṗ ṗé go ċiún ṗuṗṁúċca le feaṗ ṗ le feaṗ eile, aguṗ laḃaiṗ ṗiaḋ- le uaoiniḋ ṗiúncaċa i n-áiceaṁaiḋ ḋa aguṗ i ṗceoṗcaḃaiḋ oiṗiġeaṁla ṗṗ aṗ coṗaḋ ṁoille, moḋaḋ Ḃille Ḋáil Éipeann— " Charitable Sweep- ṁeṗ—England (Acquirement of) ṗ, 2057 A.D.", ṗé ṗin, " Ḃille ana 'Fágalcṗ Ṗeilḃe aṗ!." Tógaḋ Lán móṗ caṁnce ṗán mḂille aguṗ ṁeaḋ i ḃṗeṗóṁ é. Iṗ aṁṗṗin uo ṁeaḋ Scuaiḃin ṗuiṗṗeṁaċ ṗioṗṗṁ ṗṗing aṗ ṗiuḃal aguṗ an ṗaṗ-feaṗ nboat Gogarty i ṗcionn ṗeṁṗuiṗce.

Ḟn Scuaiḃin.

Caoḋ iṗeiṁ ḃe ṗeaċṗmain, ḃí ṫeiċ e ṗuinncṗ ḃe aiṗṗeaḋ aṗ Ṙiog ṗeilḃ Gogarty, aguṗ muinnceaṗ ana uo ċuiṗ an ċion ṗṗoṁ ḃe. ṗiṗ an c-aiṗṗeaḋ aṁ ḃoṗcaḋ iṗ ceaċ ṗóig ṗṗuc ṗleiḃe cá na ṗaiṗceanna. ḃuaiṗeanna ċṗoṁa ann. Ḃí ṗé ṗaiṗce go mḃeaḋ £15,000,000, cuṁ ṫea aṗ c-aiṗṗeaḋ aċ ḃoṗcaṗ ṗe'n ṗaṁaṁ ṗeaṗṗ i Sapana, maṗ an céaṗ ḃuaiṗ, aṗ'ṗ ṗuṗo é go ḃṗáiṗṗeaṗ oiṗeaḋ ṗṗṗo iṗ ceannṗaḋ ṗioṗaċt Sapana cuiṗṗeaṗ ṗaoi ṗmacc iṗ ṗá ṗéiṁ ṗṗeal í." Caic na h-Éiṗeannaiṗ na Scaṗmánaiṗ iṗ na Ṗṗanncaiṗ iṗ uaoime aṗ ġaċ cṗeiḋ eile aṗ an ṁan ḃoṗnán maic ḃá ṗcuṗo aṗ an aiṗḃin i ḃac an c-iomlán le céile caṗ ṁéaḋ a ḃiol Sapana ṗéin : cáinic ṁ Liúm i n-agaiḋ an ṁilliún uaṗú. leanaḋ ṗo'n ṗéiṁ go cionn ṫeiċ iaṗ go uci go ṗaḋ go ṫeoṗ ṫiṗ eile ḃoċanaṗ aguṗ an c-iomlán aiṗṗṗo aṁ cuaċca aṗ ṗeilḃ Gunboat arty.

'Sṗ Ḃéaṗla, ċeanga a ḃioḋ go ṗ ṗá ṗéiṁ i n-Éipinn ṗaḋó. aiṗe.: " Sapana ! aguṗ caḋ cuiṗe, i n-ainm hucca náṗ ċeannaiṗ

Cáinic lá an Cappaing e. Ḃí an caċaiṗ ṗlimuiṗṗe o ḃun go ḃáṗṗ le Sapanaiṗ aguṗ ṗomploí coimiṗceaṗa ḃe ġaċ cineaḋ aṗ ḃṗuim na cṗuinne. Ḃí cencṗe cnáṁa iṗ ḃpacaiṗ iṗ ṗeiṗṗ ann ó lá go maṗuim. Ḃí longa móṗa ṗan aiṗeaṁ opcṗ 'na ṗeaṗaṁ iṗ ag lionaḋ ṫaċ ḃeop ṗaiṗṗe ṗá'n céaṗpaiṗ aguṗ ḃí ṫaċ nṗo aguṗ ṫaċ neaċ aṗ ċiṗ aguṗ aṗ muiṗ ṗá ṗṗeaṁ iṗ ṗá ṗleoṗpeiṗ. Ḃí an ṗṗuim móṗ i ḃṗaiṗe an Fionn- uiṗce aguṗ ḃí ṗé leaċ-ṁile aṗ ṗaḋ, aguṗ oiṗeaḋ capaí ḃeaġa aṗ ṗaċuṗ naoi n-uaiṗe móṗ-ċimpeall an ḃoṁain ḃá ṗcuiṗṗṁḋe i ṗcionn a céile iaṗ.

Cappaingeaḋ na ḃuaiṗeanna, aguṗ ṗuaiṗ Alḃanaċ móṗ cnáṁoċ an céaṗ ḃuaiṗ aguṗ leaḃ móṗ ḃe Sapana. Cappaingeaḋ na mion-ḃuaiṗeanna. Cuiṗeaḋ nóca cuiṗ Sapana ag iaṗṗaiṗ uiṗcí ṗuim aiṗṗiṗ 'aimmiuṗ. Tionólaḋ cṗuinniú ṗṗeiṗialta ḃe'n Ṗaiṗliméiṗ aguṗ an Ṙí i ṗceannaṗ aguṗ aimmiṗeaḋ capṗ aiṗṗiṗ náṗ cualaċaṗ aṗiaṁ ḃo'n cluaiṗ ḃaonna. Ġlacaḋ leiṗ Diaṗ uaoim, Ḃealcaine 5aḋ, 2069, aguṗ ḃí pléaṗaca ionṗancaċa i mḂaile Áċa Cliac an oṗóce ṗin ḃe cineál naċ ḃṗeicceaṗ aċ go ṗioṗ annaṁ aṗ an ṗaoġal ṗeo. Cuiṗeaḋ copón aṗ ċeann Gunboat Gogarty maṗ Áṗo-Ṙí na h-Éipeann aguṗ Tiġeaṗna Sapana.

Ṙiaġalcaṗ Éiṗeannaċ i Sapana.

Cuiṗeaḋ Sapana láiṗṗeaċ aṗ ṗeilḃ na nṖáṗḃa aguṗ na n-óglaċ ; cuġaḋ ḃá lá ḃe ġaċ uaṗal aguṗ uuine ṗiúnceaċ Sapanaċ a ċiṗ, a ċuṗo callaṗó aguṗ ḃiṗnciṗe ḃo cṗéiṗṗeaḋ aguṗ ṗlanaḋ leiṗ " go h-Iṗṗionn nó go Aiméiṗiceṗ." Cuiṗeaḋ ṗcéim móṗ " Compulsory Irish " aṗ ṗiuḃal aṗ ṗuo na ċiṗe, aguṗ iṗ iomḃa ṗin aċṗú eile a cuiṗeaḋ aṗ ṗaoġal na nṖall. Ḃ'imciṗ ṗcéala ṗá'n ḃeaṗc ḃṗioġṁaṗ ṗeo go ḃċí an cuinne ḃ'iaṗṗcultṗ ḃe'n ḃoṁan ṁóṗ. Ṗpeaṗ ṫaċ ṗóṗc Sweep- stake iṗ Lotterie iṗ Scuaiḃin ṗuaṗ i nṖaċ céiṗṗ.

Scuaiḃiní Nua.

I ṗcionn camaill, cáinic ṗcéala aṁaṗ go ṗaḋ Éiṗe ceannuiṗce ag Oileán Manannáin, cé ṗuṗ ceannuiṗ luċc ṗcuaiḃin Oileán Apann Oileán Manannáin ṗéin an maṗuin céaṗoṗ. Ḃí an Seaṗmáin ag ṗóṗaiṗc a ceannuṗ aṗ an Fṗainne, aguṗ ḃí ṗúl ṗonncaḋ leaṗca ag an Spáinn aṗ Aiṗṗic Ceaṗ. Ceannuiṗ muinnceaṗ ṗṗúiṗeṗ Scuaiḃin aṗ Oileán Coṗaiṗ ceanncaṗ móṗ ḃ'Alḃam, aguṗ ḃí an c-Oileán Úp ag ḃaṗaiṗe iomlán na h-Úṗóipe ḃo ceannaṗ maṗ " ṗóṗc caḃḃaiṗce." Ḃí aiṗṗeaḋ an ḃoṁain iṗṗ na bancaṁaiḋ, ḃí ṫaċ ḃuine aċ aṁáin Gunboat Gogarty aguṗ a leiceṗoí aṗ an anáṗ, aguṗ ḃí an ḃoṁan ag ḃul ó ṗac i n-agaiḋ an lae. Ṗá ḃeiṗeaḋ ciaṗ call, cuiṗ an Ciṗ-ṗo-Ċuinn (ṗioġaċt a ceannuiṗeaḋ iṗ a ḃiolaḋ naoi n-uaiṗe), cuiṗ ṗí ṗaiṗm cum comaṗla amaċ. Cáinic na naiṗiḋin le céile, aguṗ ṗocṗuiṗeaḋ ḃeiṗeaḋ a cuṗ leiṗ an ḃṗoc-obaiṗ ṗul a ṗaḋ ḃioġḃáil a céile ḃéanca aṗ ṗao acu. Ṙinneaḋ aṁlaiḋ, aguṗ ṗágaḋ aṗiṗ ṫaċ nṗo maṗ a ḃioḋ.

Aguṗ caill Éiṗe, ṗaṗaoiṗ, a ṗealḃ aṗ Sapana.

---

ly skipping the lectures of Douglas Hyde, who (O'Nolan claimed) spoke bad Irish anyway.

Yet it was also at college that he started the lifelong habit of working intensively for short periods, an hour and a half a day, and found that he could easily get through his work by sticking to his regime. The same period of time sufficed the narrator of *At Swim-Two-Birds* to pass his exams at the conclusion of the novel. But his Bachelor of Arts degree, conferred in 1932, was not the end of his college career.

O'Nolan's bid for the auditorship of the L and H in the spring of that year suggests that it was then his intention to spend the following year in Ireland. In the event of his defeat he went to Germany instead. He had not broken his connection with UCD, however, for his name remained on the college role as candidate for the degree of Master of Arts, which he planned to take on his return from the Continent.

The battle of the sexes, as seen by O'Nolan in another cartoon of the period *(top facing previous page).*

Pissoir on the Liffey, a charming relic of the Eucharistic Congress of 1932 *(bottom facing previous page).*

Brian O'Nolan on his graduation *(previous page).*

Forms for O'Nolan's First Arts examination with odd corrections *(opposite).*

One of O'Nolan's first ventures into journalism, while still a student *(this page).*

Deutsche
Landschaft

A German Interlude

O'Nolan's visit to Germany in 1933 is a mysterious episode in his life, which may be of far greater significance than has yet been realised.

Where he went and for how long is not clear, even to his family, but there is no doubt that he went and that Germany had some special hold upon him. We know this because he refers to it in interviews and articles over a period of thirty years. Only a little time before his death he wrote in 1965 a short biographical account (the only one of its kind) for an American reference book, in which he devoted two out of eleven sentences to Germany and his feelings about the country and its people.

Those feelings were real enough. The mystery is what lay behind them.

In retrospect it was an odd year to go to Germany. O'Nolan disliked politics, yet Germany was then the most political country in Europe. Under the Weimar regime, Germany had been the fashionable resort of many artists and writers: the Berlin stories of Christopher Isherwood, for instance, evoke the atmosphere of those easy days in decadent Berlin. But, by the time O'Nolan arrived, that atmosphere had changed. In January 1933 Hitler had been appointed Chancellor. A new era was beginning for Germany.

Following the Reichstag fire in February — which was put down to a left-wing plot — new elections had confirmed Hitler's supremacy. Other political parties had been destroyed or had dissolved themselves. New laws had been passed against the Jews, and Hitler had been voted dictatorial powers. Across the country individual Communists were being hunted down and shot, Jews abused, Catholics excluded from power. Fear walked the streets: the SA, Hitler's special police, wandered the streets inflicting punishments at will, carving

Die Harzreise.

Nichts ist dauernd, als der Wechsel; nichts beständig, als der Tod. Jeder Schlag des Herzens schlägt uns eine Wunde, und das Leben wäre ein ewiges Verbluten, wenn nicht die Dichtkunst wäre. Sie gewährt uns, was uns die Natur versagt: eine goldene Zeit, die nicht rostet, einen Frühling, der nicht abblüht, wolkenloses Glück und ewige Jugend.—Börne.

> Schwarze Röcke, seidne Strümpfe,
> Weiße höfliche Manschetten,
> Sanfte Reden, Embrassieren—
> Ach, wenn sie nur Herzen hätten!
>
> Herzen in der Brust, und Liebe,   5
> Warme Liebe in dem Herzen—
> Ach, mich tötet ihr Gesinge
> Von erlognen Liebesschmerzen.
>
> Auf die Berge will ich steigen,
> Wo die frommen Hütten stehen,   10
> Wo die Brust sich frei erschließet,
> Und die freien Lüfte wehen.
>
> Auf die Berge will ich steigen,
> Wo die dunkeln Tannen ragen,
> Bäche rauschen, Vögel singen,   15
> Und die stolzen Wolken jagen.
>
> Lebet wohl, ihr glatten Säle!
> Glatte Herren! glatte Frauen!
> Auf die Berge will ich steigen,
> Lachend auf euch niederschauen.   20

Köln University — the old buildings where O'Nolan claimed to have studied *(opposite top).*

The German landscape which so appealed to O'Nolan from the 30s on *(opposite bottom).*

The opening of Heine's *Die Harzreise* *(this page).*

GOETHE'S FAUST 1932

TRANSLATED INTO ENGLISH
VERSE.

BY

SIR GEORGE LEFEVRE, M. D.

late physician to the British Embassy in St. Petersburg,
Fellow of the Royal College of physicians
in London etc.

SECOND EDITION.

FRANKFORT o. M.
PRINTED FOR CHARLES JUGEL.
AT THE GERMAN AND FOREIGN LIBRARY.
1843.

up the faces of their enemies with impunity and the connivance of the civil police.

And it was at this moment that O'Nolan chose to go to Köln. The attraction of Germany may have seemed quite reasonable to him then. He had been reading German at UCD, and his courses had introduced him to the classic writers of German literature, Goethe, Lessing, Schiller and Heine. In his Irish courses he had been exposed to the superb Germanic scholarship lavished on Celtic researches; and as an Irish Catholic he was naturally more attracted at first to the culture of Catholic southern Germany than to the Protestant north.

Though these facts might explain his initial interests, they do not explain the continuing attraction.

He went, so he later wrote, on a studentship to Köln University to do linguistic research. There is no record at UCD that he ever gained a travelling scholarship from that institution; and the University of Köln says it has no records of him either. It seems that it was not so much scholarship as sight-seeing that took

up his time. He wrote in 1965 that he "spent many months on the Rhineland and at Bonn, drifting away from the strict pursuit of study." He seems to have been away from 1933 to June 1934, though these dates are also uncertain.

The German universities, as he would have found in Köln and Bonn, were in a heady state. In February a purge of the Prussian Academy of the Arts had initiated a nation-wide drive in which some 15 percent of all university teachers, some 1200 dons, were dismissed. Those that remained often lectured in uniform. Ritual book burnings had begun at German universities in May 1933, following upon a Jewish boycott. Artists, writers, and scientists fled abroad. At home other critics were suppressed.

Even as a foreign student, O'Nolan was not unaffected. In one of the cities he visited he managed to get himself beaten up and thrown out of a bierkeller for making uncomplimentary remarks about Hitler: "They got me all wrong in that pub," he later told an interviewer in 1943. Yet according to John

Ryan, a politically alert person, whose family were prominent in Irish public life, Brian O'Nolan never condemned the Nazis: like many Irishmen he was ambiguous in his feelings for Britain's enemies, perhaps imagining that they might be Ireland's friends. Alert to many absurdities in life, O'Nolan was nevertheless politically naive.

The end of O'Nolan's first visit to Germany coincided with the "Night of the Long Knives", when Hitler turned on his henchman Rohm and the SA which he led, and ruthlessly destroyed them, murdering 1000 people in a few days.

O'Nolan seems to have been unperturbed, as he went again to Germany. 1933 had been a year of upheaval. The years between 1934 and 1938 were, in contrast, almost normal, especially in the Olympic year of 1936, when special efforts were made to impress visitors from abroad with the glories of Hitler's New Order: all that had been vicious and decadent under the old democratic government had been swept away and replaced by vigour, health and technical advance.

In these years O'Nolan returned to Germany on his holidays, a fortnight or so in the summer months. One of these was with an old college friend, John Dunne, who lived near him in Blackrock. As O'Nolan wrote in 1965; "In later years I got to know Berlin very well, and had a deep interest in the German people." He told Devin A. Garrity, the Irish-American publisher, of his visits to Berlin. In his column for the Carlow newspaper the *Leinster Nationalist* he admitted that he knew the Rhineland better than he knew the Vale of Avoca; and a Flann O'Brien letter in the *Irish Times* in the summer of 1940 joked about having his bicycle mended in Germany the year before.

In that brief biographical note the attention given to Germany is out of all proportion to the length of the piece, especially as many other important facts are passed over in silence. Can O'Nolan have been signposting a by-way in his life that no-one has since cared to explore?

Was the real attraction of Germany something more personal than the poetry of Heine, the philosophy of Kant and the operas of

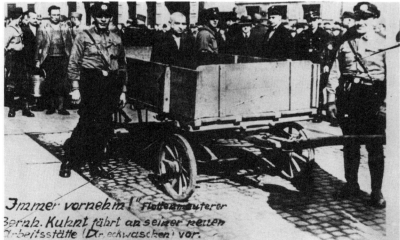

Hitler at Gera in September 1931, soon after the Nazis won power in Thuringia *(opposite left).*

The title page of O'Nolan's copy of Goethe's *Faust* *(opposite right).*

Police in Berlin rounding up Communist suspects after the Nazi take-over *(top).*

A legless veteran shortly before being murdered by the Nazis as a suspected Communist *(bottom).*

Richard Wagner?

That interview of 1943, one of very few that O'Nolan ever gave, may contain a clue. Stanford Lee Cooper, a senior editor of the magazine, published in *Time* a long profile of O'Nolan, in which he marked out his trip to Germany as the one real landmark in an otherwise uneventful life. In later years Dublin friends of O'Nolan spoke knowingly of this article as if it were a complete joke, a hoax by Myles na Gopaleen on the unsuspecting American. In his column Myles later supported this idea. And his brother Ciaran went out of his way to deny the claim about O'Nolan informally defeating the World Chess Champion Alekhine — though this is by no means an impossibility, for in those days O'Nolan carried a portable chess set with him everywhere. Yet it is clear that many people who laugh about it, know the article only by repute and have never read it.

A careful examination of the article shows that everything Cooper wrote was true; that he knew things about O'Nolan that Dublin has forgotten, especially about his civil service career. For O'Nolan the article was a sensitive issue. It exposed his real identity, which he had been at pains to deny publicly, for as a civil servant he was not supposed to publish anything without the permission of his superiors. The article was in fact cut out and added to the confidential material in his personal file with an annotation from his immediate superior John Garvin. That Cooper was accurate about what can be checked, inspires confidence in believing him about what cannot.

Cooper calls the German visit a "notable incident", mentions that O'Nolan had gone there to study the language and refers to the beer hall incident. Then he adds about O'Nolan:

He also met and married 18-year-old Clara Ungerland, blonde, violin-playing daughter of a Cologne basket weaver. She died a month later. O'Nolan returned to Eire, and never mentions her.

To his friends in Dublin, familiar from college on with O'Nolan as an ascetic misogynist, the thought of him marrying at all was a joke, let alone him marrying the blonde, violin-playing daughter of a Köln basket weaver. That had to be a joke.

O'Nolan himself referred to this report twenty years later in *Cruiskeen Lawn*, and made fun of it as a ludicrous invention. But the details he recalls from the article, that he had

O'Nolan was a pale-faced, bucktoothed youngster of 23 when he scudded into Eire's Civil Service on a foam of brilliant answers to such questions as "How far is the earth from the moon?" Born in Northern Ireland's County Tyrone, he had lived until then without notable incident save a visit to Germany in 1933.

There he went to study the language, managed to get himself beaten up and

SNOW GAUGE
Nitwits get the bucket.

bounced out of a beer hall for uncomplimentary references to Adolf Hitler: "They got me all wrong in that pub." He also met and married 18-year-old Clara Ungerland, blonde, violin-playing daughter of a Cologne basket weaver. She died a month later. O'Nolan returned to Eire, and never mentions her.

The notorious *Time* magazine version of O'Nolan's German visit — with snow gauge *(above).*

Nuremberg Party Rally *(opposite).*

married the girl on a Rhineland cruise, and that she died of galloping consumption, are not ones mentioned by Cooper. Perhaps they formed part of the original story he told the American. Or perhaps not.

A check has been made in the marriage records at Köln, but no trace has been found of an O'Nolan marriage. Viktor Böll, the son of the German novelist Heinrich Böll (who translated *The Hard Life* into German with his wife) has also checked the records independently, without success.

So just as there are no records of O'Nolan attending Köln University, there are no records of him marrying. The lack of any record is not final proof that there was no marriage, or no relationship. Perhaps his Dublin cronies are right, and the marriage was a joke and never took place. But if it did it would explain the hold that Germany had on O'Nolan, and which he underlined in such an odd manner shortly before he died.

It is curious that "Clara Ungerland" is said to have played the violin, as O'Nolan himself

did. Music, of course, would have provided a natural link between the young people. There is a musical line connecting his childhood with his late ambition (as recalled by John Ryan) of writing a Wagnerian opera on the theme of *The Palatine's Daughter*, the old Irish ballad that recounts the love of a young Irishman for the daughter of a German, albeit one settled in Ireland in the 18th century. Those German settlers had come to Ireland from the Rhineland Palatinate, just to the north of Köln.

Can O'Nolan have been using an oblique literary reference to express his inner emotions — a tactic he often resorted to?

O'Nolan continued to visit Germany. His younger brother Michael recalls his mysterious holidays, for which little explanation was given. Few people would have found much pleasure in touring Nazi Germany, unless some deep personal connection brought them there. But this is speculation.

O'Nolan seems, through the characters of Flann O'Brien and Myles na Gopaleen, so united to Dublin and Dublin life, that this

UNIVERSITÄT ZU KÖLN
UNIVERSITÄTSARCHIV

Albertus-Magnus-Platz
5000 Köln 41
Telefon (02 21) 470XXXX 3342

Köln-Lindenthal, den 12. 8. 1986

Abt.: _____ Az.: _____73_____

Es wird gebeten, im Antwortschreiben Datum
und dieses Aktenzeichen anzugeben.

          Herrn
          Dr. Peter van de Kamp
c/o   University College Dublin
          Dept. of English
          Belfield
          Dublin 4
          Ireland

Sehr geehrter Herr Dr. van de Kamp,

          Ihr an den Herrn Rektor der Universität zu Köln
gerichtetes Schreiben vom 26. Juli 1986 wurde zuständigkeits-
halber an das Universitätsarchiv weitergeleitet.
Zu meinem Bedauern muß ich Ihnen mitteilen, daß Brian O'Nolan
(O'Nuallain) in den hiesigen Matrikeln der von Ihnen angegeben
Jahre nicht ermittelt werden konnte.

Ich erlaube mir, diesem Brief einige Broschüren über die Universität zu Köln beizufügen und verbleibe mit freundlichen Grüs-
sen

                                   I.A.

                                   (G. Schütz)
                              Staatsarchivamtsrätin

German episode looks merely like a brief interlude in his life. But brief though it was it left its mark on him, to be referred to in later years. Here it must remain a mystery, in the absence of documented evidence an area for mere speculation, representing in a way the other mysteries of life of Brian O'Nolan that still defy the researcher.

The University of Köln disclaims O'Nolan — the mystery remains *(above).*

Dr Coffey, President of UCD *(opposite).*

A Novel on Pink Paper

On his return from Germany O'Nolan went back to his studies at UCD. He had already done the three terms of work which were required for his MA course. All he had to do now was to complete and present his thesis.

His subject was "Nature in Irish Poetry", and the thesis consisted of a long essay on the use of natural imagery in Irish poetry from the earliest time up to the work of quite recent writers, supported by an anthology which gathered together the examples discussed in the essay.

The material was culled from printed sources, and no original research on the manuscripts was done by O'Nolan. The essay itself saw the use of nature in Irish poetry as an important factor, not for any decorative reason but for its own sake. There was no pathetic fallacy in the Celtic mind. Nature was nature, man was man. The Celtic, and by extension, the Irish appreciation of the wilderness was pure and aesthetic. The detached and impersonal nature of the poetry he was discussing has, as the readers of his novels will see, a bearing on the writings of Flann O'Brien. He has in essence the same detachment that O'Nolan admired in the early monastic poets.

The thesis was finished in August 1934. But to his astonishment it was rejected by his tutor Agnes O'Farrelly. O'Nolan had it seems taken himself for granted. His essay had turned out to be a sentimental appreciation without critical acumen. O'Nolan had expressed himself, and forgotten that he was undertaking an academic exercise. Agnes O'Farrelly clearly felt that the essay as it then stood lacked scholarly rigour.

To his close friends O'Nolan joked about this reversal, but according to his friend Niall Sheridan he did not discuss the matter in detail. He claimed he would merely retype the thesis on pink paper and send it in again.

Among his friends this was long a joke, and has passed into the academic folklore of UCD. But in fact O'Nolan had to do more than that. He rewrote and expanded the essay, and made some revisions in the anthology. Certainly it was all typed out again on pink paper, but he was not prepared to admit that, having failed his MA, he also had to do the work all over again.

To re-enter for the MA, he had to obtain the permission of the President of the College, Dr Coffey, who gave him a letter allowing him to do so without paying a further set of fees for another year — a burden which his father, however indifferent he may have been to his children going to college, would have finally baulked at. He was also granted special permission by the Celtic faculty to use the department's own library, a distinct privilege in the circumstances.

The thesis was re-presented in August 1935 and was now found acceptable. This debacle and the kindness with which he was treated by Agnes O'Farrelly, Professor Douglas Hyde and Dr Coffey, clarifies the real meaning of the references to their "hearts of gold" in a memoir of his college years written in 1954. The facts about this episode have not been made public before, and cast a curious light on the "brilliant" O'Nolan at UCD. Brilliant he certainly was, but not in a manner that would have gained him the academic position — similar to his uncle's — for which his MA must have been the intended preparation.

But while O'Nolan had been working on his thesis, he had not been concentrating exclusively on his MA. Between August 1934 and January 1935, he had edited a satirical magazine called *Blather*, of which 6 issues appeared. This was not a college publication, but a commercial venture, published from an office in chambers at 68 Dame Street, in the business heart of the city. It was financed while it lasted by advertisements garnered from friends in business and advertising. While the aim of the journal was to entertain, O'Nolan's own intentions must have been serious. If successful it would have provided him with a journalistic base. For him it was a continuation of his college journalism through his own paper.

The magazine was largely written and illustrated by O'Nolan, who was not above including material which had previously been used in *Comhthrom Feinne*. Instead of Brother Barnabus, he invented a new persona, the Count O'Blather, who with his son Blazes O'Blather, was mostly concerned with selling a new wonder drug, Scramo.

Blather ('The Only Paper Exclusively De-

MA Degree exam form *(top)*.

O'Nolan shared the Celtic poets' love of nature *(bottom)*.

Cover of *Blather,* O'Nolan's satirical magazine, with Hitler and de Valera *(opposite left)*.

"Serenade" — O'Nolan's college poem refers to Cruiskeen Lawn *(opposite right)*.

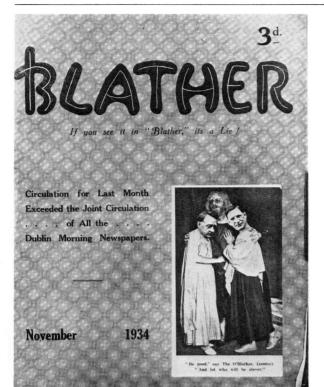

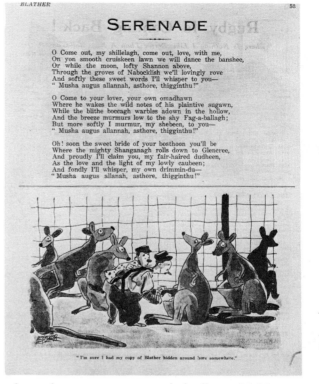

voted to the Interests of Clay-Pigeon Shooting in Ireland') began well. It was, an editorial announced, "a publication of the Gutter, the King Rat of the Irish Press, the paper that will achieve entirely new levels in everything that is contemptible, despicable and unspeakable in contemporary journalism." It belonged to that same stable of journals as *National Lampoon* and *Private Eye*: "*Blather* Doesn't Care."

But the magazine did not last into the new year. O'Nolan discovered that the patience of friends with money does not last forever. Perhaps the satire was striking in too many directions at once to build up an audience, and the opposition of the long established *Dublin Opinion* would have been hard to overcome. But it had served him well. O'Nolan had put off the troublesome business of earning his living as long as possible — where a friend like Niall Sheridan got his MA in four years, O'Nolan took six years to finish his. If an academic career was now excluded, and his own magazine had folded, there was in those harsh days after the depression, only one choice for a university man to make. He would have to follow his father into the civil service.

But these years of procrastination, as is so often the case, were artistically valuable to O'Nolan. They gave him time to acquaint himself with a range of modern authors, and to make his first efforts at writing his own novel.

Niall Sheridan, in a memoir of O'Nolan at this time, mentions some of the writers whom O'Nolan and his friends admired: Joyce and Sam Beckett, and from abroad, Hergeseimer, Cabell, Dos Passos, Hemingway, and Scott Fitzgerald. There were also the great Russians, and Proust, Kafka and Kierkegaard. These last three were, he says, of special interest to O'Nolan.

Reading was not enough, however, they wanted themselves to write. Aside from their own personal stories and poems, there was an extraordinary joint-project. O'Nolan, fresh from his magazine activities, suggested one evening in Grogan's pub in Lower Leeson Street, that Niall Sheridan, Donagh MacDonagh (poet son of the executed 1916 patriot), Denis Devlin (later Irish ambassador to Italy) and he should concoct between them the Great Irish Novel. For his own section of this saga, which dealt with the first Irishman to become Pope, he ransacked the exotic Catholicism of Baron Corvo's *Hadrian VII. Children of Destiny*, as it was to be called in a take-off

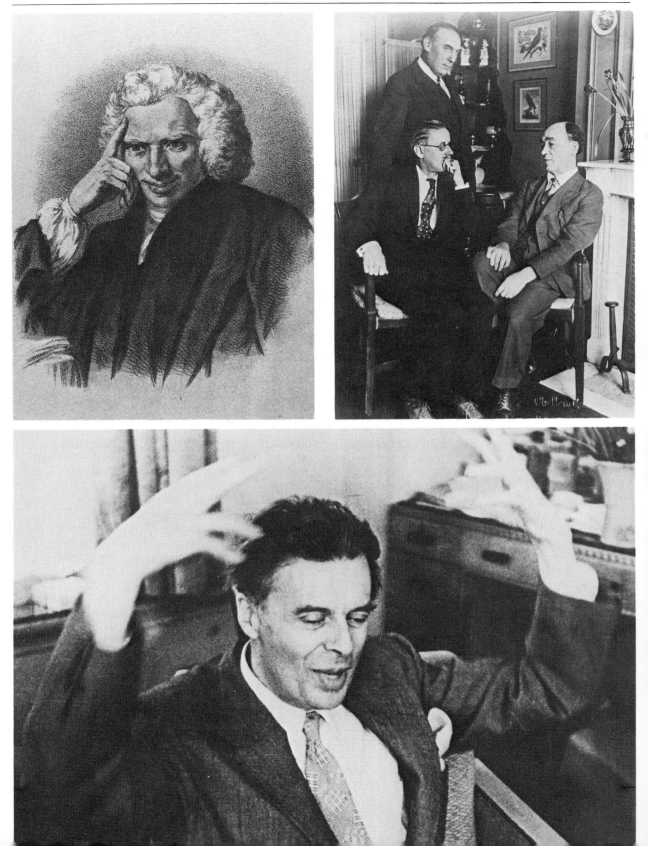

Evening Telegraph, 22/6/1932

Aistear Pheadair Dhuibh

BRIAN UA NUALLÁIN DO SCRÍOBH

RUGADH Peadar Dubh i dtoigh bheag ghlan imeasg na mónadh, eadar na sléibhte is an mhuir ; an cineál toighe a chífeá agus tú ag tabhairt an bhóthair siar ó Cheap a' Mhadaidh agus tú ag tarraingt ar Alt a' Chait—teach beag ceann-toigheadh aol-bhán aoibhinn, 'na shuidhe go sásta i n-ascal a' ghleanna. Gan amhras, ní'l gleann ar bith ag Ceap a' Mhadaidh ná ag Cúl an Bhobaire ná ag Chros-bealaigh na gCúig nGeach ach oiread ; ní'l dadaigh ann acht móin. Acht teach a bhí ann de'n chineál a tchí an fíor-Ghaedhilgeoir i gcomhnaidhe 'sa ghleanntán sléibhe agus é ag tabhairt an bhóthair siar.

Ní rabh seanchaidhe dall damhda 'na chomhnuidhe ann (mar ba cheart go mbeadh), acht, mar adubhramar thuas, Peadar Dubh agus a mháthair, bain-treabhach a chonnaic seal maith de'n tsaoghal.

Maidean amháin agus Peadar 'na thachrán ag súgradh fá'n ghríosaigh agus é ag teacht go mall i n-inmhe a chéille agus a chainnte, chraith sé a chuid meisnigh i gcionn a chéile, ghluais sé treasna an urláir agus stáin amach an doras ar a cheanntar dúthchais. Chonnaic sé portách dodach donn ag leathnadh siar go bun na spéire.

" Go bhfóiridh Dia orainn," arsa Peadar, " tá an domhan donn."

D'imthigh an aimsear agus tháinic an lá nuair sheasaigh Peadar ar a bhonnaibh féin. Is minic a rachadh sé amach ag turtáil is ag tiomsú fá'n phortach ar ghaobhar a thoighe ; gheobhadh sé dartán cruaidh colgach mónadh annseo, cionn bog brocach annsiúd, agus mór an greann aige dá gcruinniú. Bláthanna beaga aisteacha fosta, agus bataí agus smutáin mhóra bhána de ghiumhais mhónadh. Bheireadh sé an t-iomlán arais chuig a mháthair agus leoga gur minice bualadh a bhí i ndán dó ná buidheachas ós ucht a shaothair.

Is iomdha uair a chuireadh a mháthair ar a glún é, an tan a bheadh néaltaí doicheallacha dubha na h-oidhche ag leathadh a mbrat ndorcha anuas, agus síon sáileach na fairrge ag séideadh scamaill de cheo chianmhar chíotach isteach ar fud na mónadh.

" A Pheadair," adeireadh sí, " bí fabharthach i gcomhnaidhe do'n Phortach, bí maith dó agus bí carthannach. Má bhíonn tú mar chara do, ní bheidh a dhath de cheilg Ann i dtaca duit, agus ní dhéanfaidh sé dochar duit le linn do shóluis. Acht go bhfóiridh na naoimh uilig ar neamh ort an lá a chailleas tú caradas an Phortaigh. An nídh is fearr mar chara, is measa mar námhaid. Fada cuimhne an Phortaigh . . ."

* * * * * *

D'imthigh na bliadhantaí agus mhéaduigh Peadar Dubh. D'fhág sé leac an dorais agus shiubhail sé an bealach mór a bhí ag casadh go cráidhte ar fud an Phortaigh. Mhothuigh sé rudaí úra ar an tsaoghal, carraigreacha loma, fir urradhanta áireacha agus hataí móra dubha ar a gcionn ; tighthe beaga eile

Fir urradhanta díreacha agus hataí móra dubha ar a gcionn.

agus teach-pobail, cladach agus fairrge agus iasgaireacht. . . . Níor bhfada go rabh sé ar dhuine comh dána agus comh cainnteach is mhair ariamh ar an bhaile sin.

Laurence Sterne, an early model for O'Nolan *(opposite top left).*

James Joyce with James Stephens, twin influences on the modernism and folklore of *At Swim-Two-Birds* *(opposite top right).*

Aldous Huxley, another literary god of the period in UCD *(opposite bottom).*

O'Nolan cartoon of giants from the period, recalling the spirit of the novel *(above).*

An early article in Irish satirising the peasant glamour of the day *(bottom).*

Advertisement for what may have been the original of the Red Swan Hotel in *At Swim-Two-Birds* (top).

W. B. Yeats introducing George Moore to the Queen of the Fairies — Max Beerbohm's famous drawing mocks as O'Nolan does the feyness of the Literary Revival (bottom).

MA degree form for the thesis that caused too much trouble (opposite top).

Cowherding through the streets of Dublin, for long a familiar scene (opposite bottom).

A novel on pink paper: pp. 79 and 80 of the mss of *At Swim-Two-Birds* typed on similar paper to his thesis (following page).

M.A. DEGREE.

I desire to be examined in the following Subjects.......................

....

The Candidate must here state clearly the Mode under which he
intends to present himself.

Mode IA

"Nádúip-pilíocz na Zaedilze".

Prof. O'Farrelly, M.A.

CERTIFICATE OF ATTENDANCE ON COURSES.

(To be signed at EACH entry by the Registrar of the College of which you
are a student).

This is to certify that...*Brian Ó Nualláin*...
is attending, or has attended, in this College, Courses in the Subjects
specified above, these being the Courses required for the foregoing
Examination ; and that his attendance has been satisfactory.

Registrar of *University College (Dublin)*

* For Candidates entering for the M.A. Degree on Research under
Statutes VIII. and X., it will be necessary to comply with the following
requirements of Senate :—

That Abstracts, in duplicate, of 100 to 300 words of Dissertations
by Candidates for Degrees on Research, must be lodged with the
Registrar, The National University of Ireland, 49 Merrion Square,
Dublin C.17.

of the national anthem (*Soldiers of Destiny*)
came to nothing. But as a working method,
the ransacking of other men's literature to
parodic purpose would remain a common
device with O'Nolan.

Niall Sheridan was now the editor of *Comhthrom Feinne*. O'Nolan wrote for him the
beginning of a serial, written in Middle Irish,
about the activities of students in Dublin in the
manner of Boccaccio. There would be no
trouble about it, he said, as only two or three
of the most eminent scholars in the university
would be able to read it. Nevertheless, after
the appearance of the first episode, Sheridan
was summoned to the President's office. Dr
Coffey charged him with the curious offence of
publishing obscene matter in Old Irish. But as
it transpired that neither of them could read
the offending prose, they passed politely on to
other topics. Sheridan departed at the end of
the interview with £25 for reviving the Chess
Club, of which he made O'Nolan president.
He made himself treasurer.

During the summer of 1935 O'Nolan tried
his hand at broadcasting, giving fortnightly
talks on books to the audience of the Irish
radio service (the director of which had been
newly recruited from the faculty of UCD). But
he had also a more important project in hand:
his own first novel.

In June of that year, as Brian O'Nolan was
completing his thesis on pink paper, Sheridan
was able to inform the readers of *Comhthrom*

X
like boys because Flanagan would
think nothing of shooting the lights out
I no, that's the truth. (You had a
right to go for the police). That's the very
thing we done.

it a good start in life and such deference as will save it somme
from the inducements of showmen and cross-mappers.

—You dirty dog, says I between my teeth, you dirty swine you,
Flanagan, you bastard. *(You had good reason to be. If I was there I don't know what I do and that's a fact)* We don't was in a right temper, and that's
a fact.   Wait till Tracey hears about it says I, noble big-hearted
Tracey that refused to hear *us* even pieces behind the bloody
scullery door.   But lord save us, I might as well talk to the
sweet wall.   One thing *He gave three minutes to go home and how we want* X
to another one *at the heel of the hunt the* Tensora came out
and crowded round and _____ three of
us found ourselves bound and gagged, hand and foot, and shagged into
(that was a nice how do you do)
a dirty filthy stab, thrown on our knees on *the floor* _____.
After laughing at us and scattering about for a while, smoking
Mexican cigarettes, and telling each other that you can't beat a
good nigger nativ, for the hard stuff and us lying there listening,
in went the whole crowd of them to the bunkhouse and shut the door
and took to shouting and singing and whistling like be damned.
If we don't get to hell out of this dungsty before sunup, says I
dirty
told — gag, it'll be *(You don't mean that?) Every word of it*
____ free to-morrow morning, says I.   After a good hour of
hard thinking, I felt — *men* — nibbling at my ankles.   I gave
a kick and looked round and _____ *here was* Slug and his
teeth, the picture-card that was round me with his _____ spur.
(He had plenty of gumption the same man,)   you
Do you mind the cleverness of it! _____
_____
god save the mark, and his educated training, you know, was standing
in the — for the lot of us in our hour of need.
Mang first, thinks I, and slithered round till my wrist-cords

_____ *Patul Sheridan. comes in 1500*

Feinne that O'Nolan was at work on a novel "so ingeniously constructed that the plot is keeping him well in hand." In fact he was writing it on the same pink paper as his thesis, and inevitably bits of the thesis made their way into the book. As they were completed O'Nolan showed his friend sections of the book, in which Sheridan was astonished to realise he was a character along with Finn MacCool, and a host of characters largely drawn from existing books. He was, of course, the narrator's friend, Brinsley.

As it progressed O'Nolan added to the script whatever came to hand: a conversation with the painter Cecil French Salkeld became the basis of the visit to Michael Byrne; a Catullus translation by Sheridan (later to be included in the *Oxford Book of Irish Verse* which was edited by Donagh MacDonagh) was copied verbatim; an encounter in Lad Lane on Conferring Night in 1934, when one of their friends was sick over a gentlemen who had accosted them; a circular from a bookmaker in England.

At Swim-Two-Birds was a book which contained three other books, and entailed a vertiginous transition from style to style. The title of the book — an actual place on the River Shannon — and much of the material was taken from *The Madness of Sweeney*, a Middle Irish text from which O'Nolan had culled many verses for his thesis. Other material came from the myth of Finn and the

Michael Victor Nolan, the father in later years *(top)*.

Father photographed by street photographer shortly before his death *(bottom)*.

4 Avoca Terrace, today with memorial plaque *(opposite)*.

Fianna, also studied by O'Nolan. But around the tragedy of King Sweeney turned by magic into a bird, he was able to weave a web of narrative effects which drew on every strand of his literary experience. He raided literature for his material, rebuilding what he took into a new and fantastic edifice.

In the context of Irish literature what he was doing was something completely new, equalled only in a very different way by Joyce in *Finnegans Wake*. Other writers had made use of legendary and literary material, but all had written with an eye on the conventions of the Irish literary revival. For Brian O'Nolan the Irish revival did not exist, or if it did, it was some kind of fraud. He was not writing as part of a national tradition. He was writing pure literature.

Like his narrator, O'Nolan worked at home, at 4 Avoca Terrace. There in an upstairs room looking out over the park in front of the house, he wrote *At Swim-Two-Birds*, *The Third Policeman*, and the original version of *An Beal Bocht*. He had made his work table for himself, using as legs the supports of an old garden trellis. That original trellis entered directly into the novel in the person of Dermot Trellis. The home life of the narrator in the book suggests something of the life O'Nolan lived as a student from 1929 to 1935, though doubtless he was less dirty and unkempt. His relations with his father would have been as distant as those of the narrator with his "uncle".

The book was more or less complete in 1935. But it was never intended for publication. This was because O'Nolan had entered the civil service in the summer of 1935, and had inevitably little time even for part-time literary activities. In fact he published nothing between 1935 and 1938. Indeed he would never have taken up a writing career if his father had not died suddenly on 29 July, 1937.

He had been playing with his youngest child Niall when he suffered a brain haemorrhage. Brian was with him when he passed away on the floor of the drawing room. The sombre conclusion of *At Swim-Two-Birds*, which was written in October 1938 to replace an earlier ending, and which strikes such a different note to much of what had gone before, owes something to the shock which O'Nolan sustained by his father's death. It was an event which altered the tenor of his life completely. In the summer of 1937 he had suddenly to grow up.

His father died leaving little over £550 — less even than James Joyce's spendthrift father. Mrs Nolan was left in very difficult circumstances. Ciaran, the eldest, was now working as a journalist but poorly paid; Roisin was teaching; Brian was in the civil service. All the others were either at college or in school. The support of this large family revolved upon Brian. He paid for their rearing, their education, and when the time came, paid for the girls' weddings. He was, his brother Michael remarks, a father of twelve without the experience.

Until now O'Nolan had been very much the model civil servant. His father's will was probated by Brian in September 1937 and the serious financial situation facing the family was only too clear. There was only one easy solution, he would have to add to his salary by writing.

What he had to hand were some college pieces and the script of his novel. He sent an article in Irish, an extract from a student novel, to *Ireland Today* where it was published in February 1938. By January of that year he had a complete version of *At Swim-Two-Birds* ready. He had shown the book again to Niall Sheridan, who advised him to remove from it a large section (how long is now uncertain)

The hallway of the house in Avoca
Terrace with hatstand, painted by
Brian's younger brother *(above)*.

Brian O'Nolan about the time of the
publication of his novel in 1939 *(opposite
left)*.

Graham Greene, whose opinion led to
the publication of *At Swim-Two-Birds*
(opposite right).

dealing mostly with Finn MacCool. This certainly improved the book. His senior in the civil service, John Garvin, was also asked for his opinion. He too suggested revisions, and gave O'Nolan the Greek epigraph. It was from Euripides' *Hercules Furens*, "For all things go out and give place to one another."

The book was sent first to William Collins (the firm his father had sent his detective novel to), who rejected it. But Longmans, "the Catholic crowd" as O'Nolan calls them in a letter, accepted it, largely on the basis of an enthusiastic report from their reader, Graham Greene. Unlike some publishers, Greene was able to recognise the merits of the book he saw in draft. "It is in the line of *Tristram Shandy* and *Ulysses*: its amazing spirits do not disguise the seriousness of the attempt to present, simultaneously as it were, all the literary traditions of Ireland."

Further changes were made in the book, including the new ending mentioned earlier, and the novel was published on 13 March 1939. O'Nolan received an advance of £30, so it may not have quite come up to his expectations from the point of view of income. It appeared (to preserve his civil service position) under the pen-name of Flann O'Brien. A new personality was born.

The reviews were puzzled, but in the main enthusiastic. Dylan Thomas recognised its merits at once. The novel, he wrote, "establishes Mr O'Brien in the forefront of contemporary writing." He looked forward to his next book. But in six months the book sold only 244 copies. Eventually Longmans' warehouse was bombed and most of the edition lost. A small number of sheets which were at the printers were bound and reissued, but the war O'Nolan felt had killed the book. The book had fallen into the stage of flux referred to in its epigraph and had to give place in turn to other books.

Niall Sheridan, who was to spend his honeymoon in Paris, took an inscribed copy of the book to James Joyce, whom he was calling on there. He was surprised to discover that the book had already been brought to Joyce's notice by Sam Beckett. Joyce was delighted with the book and its author. "That's a real writer, with the true comic spirit. A really funny book."

At the end of the year the committee awarding the AE Memorial Award (one of whom was Sean O'Faolain) gave the prize to Patrick Kavanagh, but went out of their way to make a separate special award of £30 to Flann

O'Brien.

O'Nolan had sent a copy of the book to
Ethel Mannin, a then popular novelist at the
height of her notoriety. She disliked the book
and sent him a postcard to tell him so. In reply
he disavowed the literary aspirations which
she had attributed to the book, pointing out
that he was writing stories for the Sexton
Blake library at £50 each. This was what
seemed to interest him: the money side of the
business.

The amateur with his part-time literary
activities had been forced by circumstances to
become a professional writer.

These particular Sexton Blake stories have
as yet to be identified. But they served one
permanent purpose. They suggested a murder
and its consequences as theme of a serious
Flann O'Brien novel. The actual plot of *The
Third Policeman*, the resultant novel, was, he
told his friend William Saroyan, the best thing
about the book. He thought it might make a
good play.

He fitted out his thriller, if that is what it can
be called, with an apparatus of bogus scholarship relating to the theories of the great
fictional savant de Selby. His friends were
enchanted: Niall Sheridan was impressed,
Donagh MacDonagh astonished. "It was three
quarters footnotes," he recalled.

In 1940 Longmans rejected the book. They
felt it was too unusual, and that he should
write something more ordinary, more
approachable and more acceptable to the
ordinary reader.

O'Nolan was stunned by this rejection. He
made up tales of losing it at a pub, on a drive

through Donegal, anything that came into his
mind to avoid dealing with the problem. He
hid the book at home, though in 1942 the idea
of a play based on the plot was mentioned to
Hilton Edwards of the Gate Theatre in Dublin. The great lost novel was a secret, something that remained unknown to all save his
closest friends, and even then they did not
know the whole truth of the matter.

But meanwhile money was still needed. He
had to think of something else. That trip to the
west on which he was supposed to have lost
the novel was made to provide material for a
travel book that was never written. As the
father of twelve he had the immediate needs of
the children to think about. He set about
creating, on the reputation of *At Swim-Two-
Birds*, a new career.

**Sean O'Faolain and O'Nolan about
1940 when O'Nolan was writing for
The Bell (above).**

The typescript of the novel (*opposite*).

- 184 -

the Italian operas, from the compositions of Puccini and Meyerbeer
and Donizetti and Gounod and the Maestro Mascagni as well as an
aria from The Bohemian Girl by Balfe, and intoned the choral
complexities of Palestrina the pioneer. They rendered two hundred
and forty-two songs by Schubert in the original German words, and
sang a chorus from Fidelio, *(by Beethoven, of Moonlight Sonata fame)* and the Song of the Flea, and a long
excerpt from a Mass by Bach, as well as innumerable tuneful
pleasantries from the able pen of no less than Mozart and Handel.
To the stars (though they could not see them owing to the roofage
of the leaves and the branches above them) they gave with a thunderous
spirit such pieces by Offenbach, Schumann, Saint-Saens and Granville
Bantock as they could remember. They sang entire movements from
cantatas and oratorios and other items of sacred music, *allegro ma non troppo, largo and andante cantabile.*

They were all so preoccupied with music that they
were still chanting spiritedly in the dark undergrowth long after
the sun, earlier astir than usual, had cleaned the last vestige of
the soiling night from the verdure of the leaves on the treetops, *away, for good purposes of the sacred greeny*
when they suddenly arrived to find mid-day in a clearing, they
wildly reproached each other with bitter words and groundless
allegations of bastardy as they collected berries and haws into the
hollows of their hats against a late breakfast. *the incidence of* *Temporary discontinuance of the foregoing.*
BIOGRAPHICAL ^REMINISCENCE — INSERT HERE
At twenty past four they arrived at the Red Swan
Hotel and entered the premises unnoticed by the window of the maid's
lavatory at the back on the ground floor. They made no noise in
their passage and disturbed none *dust* of the dusts that lay about the
carpets. Quickly they repaired in a body to the ante-room to Miss
Lamont's bedroom (where the lady was lying in) and deftly stacked the

the very words .... — Paul Shanahan leaving the Pooka

Flann Becomes Myles

Brian O'Nolan's literary career having run ahead of his professional life, we must go back some years to catch up on his civil service life.

O'Nolan entered the civil service in the summer of 1935. Despite his college degrees, he had still to sit the usual Civil Service Commission exam, finding (as he later recalled) brilliant answers to such questions as "How far is the earth from the moon?" He was soon to find that such general information was not required by the job.

He was attached to the Department of Local Government, in Gandon's magisterial Custom House on the quays. He was made a junior administrative officer under the personal supervision of John Garvin (better known among Joycean scholars under his pen-name Andrew Cass), then Assistant Principal Officer in the Finance Section, which dealt largely with government loans to the local authorities in rural Ireland.

The shy, even diffident 23-year-old was given his own desk in a corner of Garvin's office, where he was taught the intricate etiquette of the modern civil service. Administrative routine was no problem. But Garvin had to impress upon him that official letters were not a medium for personal expression. Restraint came with time.

Under Garvin, who became for O'Nolan a benevolent father-figure, during the years 1935 to 1937, O'Nolan or O Nuallain as he

now styled himself for official purposes, learnt "to prepare letters and minute files", leaving them punctiliously prepared for Garvin on his return to the office in the late afternoon.

Much of the work of the department was concerned with roads and drains, those dull but necessary features of the civil scene. But the central government was also taking steps towards the re-organisation of local government through the appointment of city and county managers directly responsible to the central authorities. Democracy was very nice, but Mr de Valera also believed in strong government.

Impressed by the "strength of his ability and efficiency" of the young O'Nolan, Garvin recommended him to fill the vacant post of Private Secretary to the Minister, at that time the genial Sean T. O'Kelly (later elected President of Ireland in 1946). O'Nolan was promoted to this sensitive and demanding post

in 1937, shortly after his father's sudden death. In 1937 Paddy Ruttledge became Minister, to be followed in 1934 by Sean McEntee. O'Nolan served these men with distinction.

Even from the earliest days, however, the civil service does not seem to have been congenial to O'Nolan. He had to face the credo that it was "a gentleman's service", a notion which was a hangover from the days of the British. But O'Nolan the UCD rabble-rouser was no old-fashioned civil servant, even if he dressed like one. It was this unobtrusive young man who now set about making a name for himself, not as Brian O'Nolan, but as Flann O'Brien, Myles na Gopaleen, Lir O'Connor and others.

His college friends Donagh MacDonagh and Niall Sheridan had become contributors to the *Irish Times*, MacDonagh doing pieces for the book page, and Sheridan writing a column of racing tips under the name of Birdcatcher.

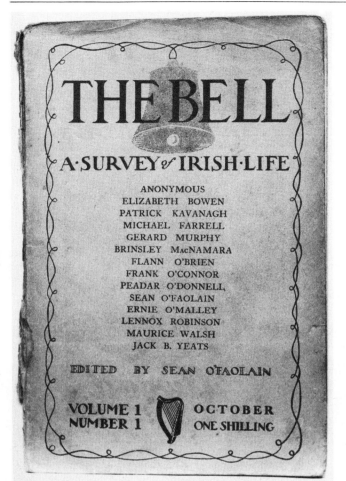

Illustration of one of De Selby's theories — an accumulation of black air taking place *(facing previous page)*.

The Customs House, with Guinness Harp *(previous page)*.

Tom Garvin, O'Nolan's new father-figure *(opposite left)*.

Sean McEntee, for many years O'Nolan's Minister *(opposite right)*.

O'Nolan among his peers — the cover of *The Bell (above)*.

Myles to the rescue — drawing by Queen Victoria of Boucicault in the part *(bottom)*.

Beachcomber's creation, Mr Thake,
which influenced O'Nolan *(top)*.

R. M. Smyllie, after hours in The Palace
(bottom).

The words and music of *Cruiskeen Lawn*
from Boucicault's play *(opposite page)*.

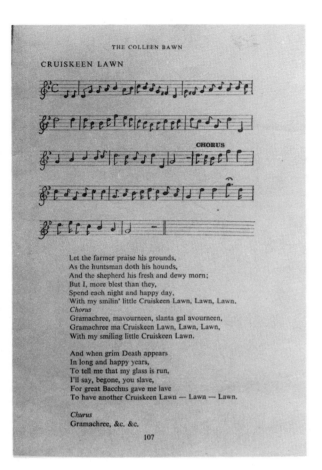

THE COLLEEN BAWN

CRUISKEEN LAWN

CHORUS

Let the farmer praise his grounds,
As the huntsman doth his hounds,
And the shepherd his fresh and dewy morn;
But I, more blest than they,
Spend each night and happy day,
With my smilin' little Cruiskeen Lawn, Lawn, Lawn.
Chorus
Gramachree, mavourneen, slanta gal avourneen,
Gramachree ma Cruiskeen Lawn, Lawn, Lawn,
With my smiling little Cruiskeen Lawn.

And when grim Death appears
In long and happy years,
To tell me that my glass is run,
I'll say, begone, you slave,
For great Bacchus gave me lave
To have another Cruiskeen Lawn — Lawn — Lawn.

Churus
Gramachree, &c. &c.

107

Though the politics of the paper were pro-British, it was in the prevailing gloom of the country at the time, a bright light. In what seems very like a concerted plot, his friends set about the task of getting O'Nolan an opening in the paper.

In January 1939 O'Nolan and Sheridan began a controversy over the merits of a play by Frank O'Connor which had been badly reviewed by the critic in the *Irish Times* and defended in a letter by Sean O'Faolain. O'Nolan and Sheridan (writing under several names) used the occasion to attack the whole school of writers which O'Connor and O'Faolain represented. Another row over the production *The Three Sisters* in January 1940 eventually ran on into another one, which began in the middle of the year, and concerned a review of a novel by Maurice Walsh which Patrick Kavanagh had contributed. This too burned itself out, but not before 20 months of letter writing had achieved the desired result.

According to Niall Sheridan, R. M. Smyllie, the editor of the *Irish Times*, was amused by these letters. He rang Sheridan and asked him to bring O'Nolan along to the Palace Bar in Fleet Street, where he held court in the inner lounge on Friday evenings. Here Sheridan's memory may be playing him false, for according to John Garvin, when *At Swim-Two-Birds* was published in March 1939, he and O'Nolan celebrated the fact in the Palace with Smyllie and his deputy editor Alec Newman. So Smyllie must have been aware of O'Nolan for nearly 2 years before he contacted Sheridan.

What brought him to his attention at such a late date in 1940 and reminded him of the fluency of O'Nolan's letters was an appearance by Flann O'Brien. Sean O'Faolain had been one of the committee that had made the special award of the AE Memorial Prize to O'Nolan. When he was preparing the first issue of his new literary magazine *The Bell* he asked O'Nolan to contribute. Using the name Flann O'Brien, he wrote two articles, one about greyhound racing and another on public houses of Dublin. The first of these appeared in the first issue of *The Bell* in October 1940. O'Brien's name was on the cover. The same month, again writing as Flann O'Brien, he contributed an eulogy of Standish O'Grady to the *Irish Times*. By then *Cruiskeen Lawn (The little overflowing Jug)* had been appearing since 4 October.

O'Nolan's versatility would have been obvious from the letters written during the controversies. His knowledge of Irish coupled with his irreverence made him the ideal person to write a column in Irish for the paper. The first article, tucked into the editorial page just under the Court Circular, was signed "An Broc" — the Badger. The second article was signed Myles na Gopaleen. It was to appear, on and off, for the next 26 years.

The pen-name was taken from Boucicault's play *The Colleen Bawn*, which was drawn from Gerald Griffin's novel *The Collegians*. In the novel *Myles* makes a brief appearance; in the play he has a leading role, created by Boucicault for himself. The play and the character represented the Stage Irishman in his worst form. O'Nolan intended it not so much as a nom de plume but as a nom de guerre.

There is no doubt that in the context of Irish journalism *Cruiskeen Lawn* was original. The readers of the paper, largely Protestant Unionists and Catholic professionals, took notice

at once. Letters of protest and praise began to arrive, a sure sign to the editor that the new column was at least being read with interest and attention.

At first *Cruiskeen Lawn* was always in Irish, and remained so until the autumn of 1943. Then English began to make its appearance, and to take up more and more space. In 1943 the *Irish Times* was able to issue a bilingual paperback of the column. But after March 1944 the column was rarely in Irish. Myles found that he wished to hit targets that required the continual use of English. Whatever Smyllie's original intentions may have been, Myles had his own ideas and became very much his own master.

Since the publication of *The Best of Myles* after O'Nolan's death, his readers outside Ireland have been able to judge for themselves the effects achieved in the column. As it developed over the years, some outside influences were detectable. An obvious one, what with the constant multilingual puns and word-

play, was Fr Prout, the 19th century comic writer. Closer to hand was the "Beachcomber" column in the London *Daily Express*, in which many of Myles' devices, such as the district court, are to be found.

J. B. Morton, who wrote the Beachcomer column, was a Catholic who had taken it over from another Catholic. The *Daily Express* was not a paper notable for its Catholic outlook. Myles, too, on the *Irish Times* was a Catholic outsider writing for an audience whose standards and outlook he did not share. As the readership of the paper widened from its pro-British base, this changed, and he was widely read by the Catholic professional and university classes.

Flann O'Brien and Myles na Gopaleen were not O'Nolan's only pen-names at this time. He also wrote lighter pieces, in a more whimsical vein, for the *Times Pictorial* under the Lir O'Connor, which he found useful as well for articles in magazines like the *Irish Digest* which did not want too much of Flann O'Brien. It is likely that much of his occasional journalism remains untraced. But these pieces, like his detective thrillers, are mere curiosities. They will not alter his literary fame.

The popularity of the column led to an

An *Irish Times* publication of a selection of the column in 1943 *(opposite left)*.

Brian O'Nolan in his heyday, drawn by his friend Sean O'Sullivan *(opposite right)*.

The cover of Tomas O Crohan's autobiography *(top)*.

The original cover of O'Nolan satire which guyed it *(bottom)*.

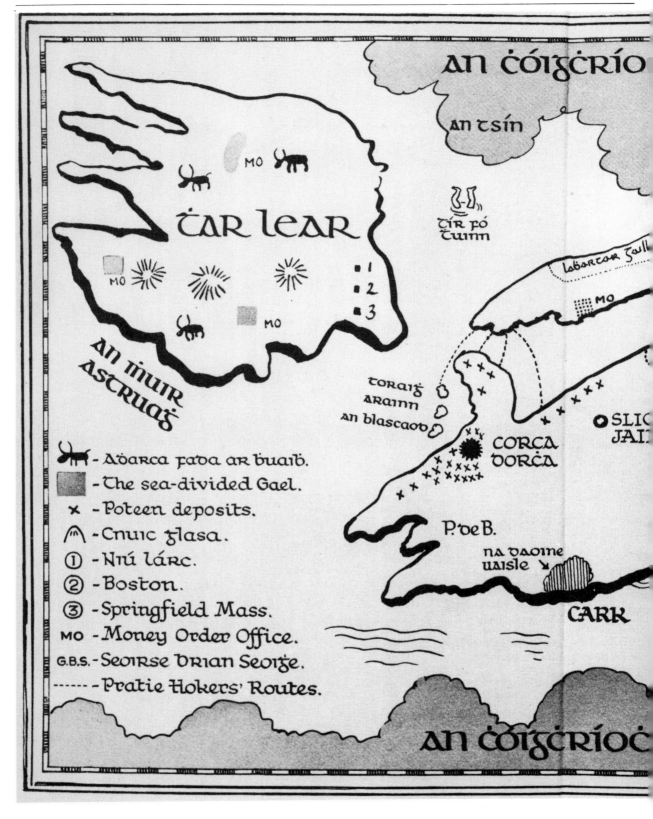

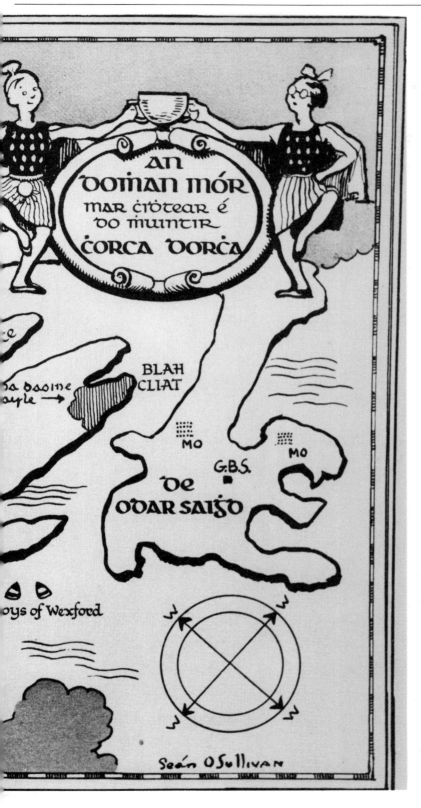

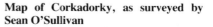

Map of Corkadorky, as surveyed by Sean O'Sullivan

Life in Corkadorky, as envisaged by
Ralph Steadman *(top)*.

Surprised by the monster on the beach
(bottom).

Tomas O Crohan, author of *The
Islandman* *(opposite top)*.

Peig Sayers, another of the Blasket
writers *(opposite bottom)*.

invitation from a small publisher for a "Myles na Gopaleen" novel. He had on hand a script which had already been rejected by Browne and Nolan, a prominent Irish publishing firm. This was *An Beal Bocht*, a biting satire on the Irish language movement written in perfect Irish.

O'Nolan had originally written the book as a response to Thomas O Crohan's book *The Islandman* when the original Irish edition had been published in 1930. He wrote it very quickly, though doubtless the book was amended later on. *An Beal Bocht* thus belongs not to 1941 when it was published, but to that short highly creative period during his college years. When it was published it was an immense success, going through two large printings, and making its way into households where an Irish language book had not been bought for years.

What O'Nolan was satirising was not O Crohan or Peig Sayers or any of the other Blasket writers. His targets were the manipulators of the language, those who had drained it of purpose, who had emasculated a strong, rich tradition, casting over the earthiness of Irish life the pall of Victorian respectability.

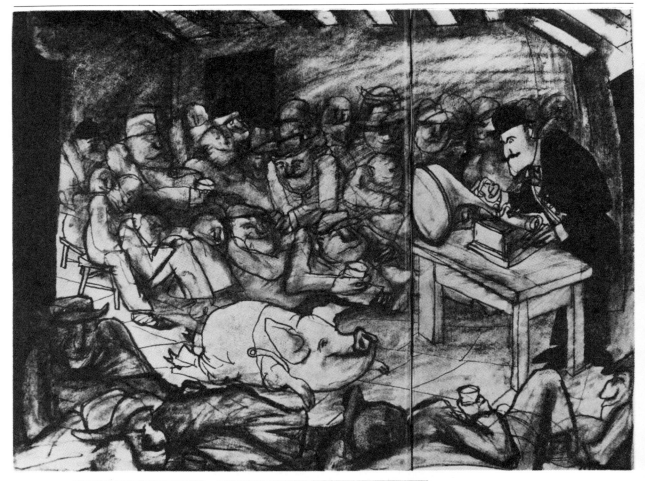

The grand hard old Irish of the pig in *The Poor Mouth* (top).

Advertisements for O'Nolan's book when it was first published (bottom).

A collector from the Irish Folklore Commission at work in the field (opposite).

Translated into English after his death, the book won new admirers as *The Poor Mouth*. But for the Irish readers, reared as Myles had been in school and college on the books of "Maire" and other Gaelic writers, the book has a rich comicality quite lost in translation.

So, slowly the Irish language faded out of the *Cruiskeen Lawn* column, and it came to be written entirely in English. Indeed Myles refused to write in Irish anymore, keeping what he wrote in that language for his brother Ciaran's paper *Inniu*.

What gave the column its peculiar power over the years was the knowing manner in which Myles would hint at secrets and scandals unknown to the wider public. He was not joking in this. O'Nolan's position as a civil servant, directly involved in the daily affairs of the government, gave Myles na Gopaleen a unique insight into the realities of Irish life. For a time his life as a civil servant was of creative use to him.

As Private Secretary to the Minister he was required to attend in the Dail, the Irish parliament, for many hours a week. In later years he would discourse on the pain of listening to the deputies sent there by the electorate. They provided an unwholesome spectacle for the young man.

On Dail paper — perhaps even while sitting in the chamber — he began to draft a play called *Faustus Kelly*, in which he transposed the scenario of Gounod's opera *Faust*, based on Goethe's original drama, to an Irish setting, making good use of his own experiences of local government. His main character was a local councillor who sells his soul to the Devil for political power, and the play made deft use of traditional Irish political rhetoric.

The play was begun in April 1942 and was typed out by 11 July. He sent the script to the Abbey, and after some changes — many of which related to his constant use or rather misuse of the Holy Name — had been agreed

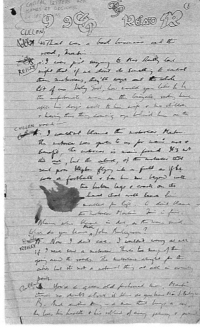

Cover of the programme for the *Jack-in-the-Box* show *(top left)*.

The original cast of O'Nolan's play *Thirst* *(bottom)*.

Page from the draft of *Faustus Kelly* *(top right)*.

Myles in the Underworld, a cartoon from the *Irish Digest* showing Myles in the *Faustus Kelly* period *(opposite)*.

JACK - IN - THE - BOX

Hilton Edwards
Micheál MacLiammóir
Dublin Gate Theatre
Productions, Ltd.

1. PRELUDE

Two Pianos	..	Úna Ní Icidhe, Marie McCrystal
Two Golliwogs	..	Tony Mathews, Teddy Lucas
Jack-in-the-Box	..	Hilton Edwards

2. THE LITTLE MATCH GIRL
(Adapted from Hans Andersen)

The Carol Singers .. Soprano: Sadie Bolger. Alto: Mairín Fenning.
Tenor: T. P. O'Brien. Bass: Thomas Peacock.

The Little Match Girl	..	Shirley Bentinck
The Sugar Plum Fairy	..	Monica Maguire
Some Children	..	Alexis Milne, Maureen Kennedy, Eileen Ashe, Collette Redmond
Three Shepherds	..	Anthony Walsh, Dermot Tuohy, James Neylin
Three Wise Men	..	Diarmuid Kelly, Christopher Casson, Val Iremonger
Our Lady	..	Findala Monaghan
Two Angels	..	Nellie O'Brien, Shiela Keddy

3. ZOO BLUES
(A Zoological Night's Entertainment)
By Micheál MacLiammóir. Music and Lyric by Tyrrell Pine.
Scene I.—The Monkey House. Scene II.—The Lion House.

Harry	.. Sean Colleary	Tamara (a Tigress)	Meriel Moore
Joe	.. William Fassbender	Rajah (a Tiger)	Liam Gaffney
Lizzie	.. Sally Travers	Lizzie (a Lioness born in the Zoo)	
Mrs. Knox	.. Sara Payne		Betty Chancellor
Jill	.. Alexis Milne	Henry (a Lion)	Robert Hennessy
A Keeper	.. Diarmuid Kelly		

Also, a Tiger and Tigress from Bertram Mills Circus, London.

4. A LADY FAIR
(From "Irish Street Ballads" by courtesy of Colm Ó Lochlainn)
Special musical setting by Dr. John Larchet.

The Lady	..	Sadie Bolger
The Sailor	..	Christopher Casson

5. THIRST
By Myles na gCopaleen
Place—A Pub in or near Dublin. Time—Gentlemen, Please!

Mr. C. (a Publican)	..	Robert Hennessy
Jim (a Customer)	..	William Fassbender
Peter (another Customer)	..	Sean Colleary
A Sergeant of the Gárda Síochána	..	Liam Gaffney

6. FOUR FLOPS
(or PLEASE MR. EDWARDS, WILL YOU TEACH ME HOW TO ACT?)
By Micheál MacLiammóir. Music and Lyrics by Tyrrell Pine.
(The scene takes place on the stage of the Gate Theatre)

The Stage Manager	..	Cecil Monson
A Few Aspirants	..	Betty Chancellor

7. LA SAINTE COURTESANE or
THE WOMAN COVERED WITH JEWELS
(A fragment by Oscar Wilde)
Music by Delius. Scene—The Desert near Alexandria.

The first Man	..	Christopher Casson
The second Man	..	Anthony Walsh
Myrrhina (a Woman of Alexandria)	..	Meriel Moore
Honorius (a Hermit)	..	Micheál MacLiammóir

8. FINNIGAN'S WAKE
(From " Irish Street Ballads," by courtesy of Colm Ó Lochlainn)
Musical setting by Tyrrell Pine. Choreography by Sara Payne.

The Balladmonger Liam Gaffney	Biddie O'Brien ..	Jean St. Clair
Tim Finnigan .. Robert Hennessy	Biddie O'Connor	Sally Travers
Paddy Magee .. Diarmuid Kelly	Neighbours ..	Alexis Milne,
Mick Molony Christopher Casson		Anthony Walsh, James Neylin,
Mrs. Finnigan Rosalind Halligan		W. Fassbender, Val Iremonger.

INTERVAL

9. INTERLUDE

Two pianos	..	Úna Ní Icidhe, Marie McCrystal

10. THE OLD SAILOR. By A. A. Milne
Scene—A Desert Island.

A Little Pet	..	Jean St. Clair
The Old Sailor	..	Christopher Casson
The Rescue Party	..	Diarmuid Kelly, Anthony Walsh

11. THE STYLISH MARRIAGE. By Micheál MacLiammóir
(BEING THE TRUE HISTORY OF DAISY BELL)
Scene I.—A Corner of St. Stephen's Green, 1942.

Diana	..	Betty Chancellor
Ozzie	..	Hilton Edwards

Scene II.—A Respectable Dublin House in the early nineties

Mr. Bell	..	Liam Gaffney
Mrs. Bell	..	Sara Payne
Daisy (their Daughter)	..	Betty Chancellor
Osmond (their namesake)	..	Hilton Edwards

Scene III.—Rapture On The Road.

with the theatre's director Ernest Blythe, it was first performed on 25 January 1943, and ran for two weeks.

The popularity of his column in the *Irish Times* had raised expectations in a crowded first night. As Myles he was a public figure — "the jester Myles". Patrick Kavanagh, in his column in *The Standard*, had given the play a friendly plug. O'Nolan's friends, superiors (such as Sean MacEntee), Patrick Kavanagh and many others were there. Rumour had it that there might be another "Abbey Row" to equal the first nights of *The Playboy of the Western World* and *The Plough and the Stars*. Madame Kirkwood Hackett and her son were there with other Republicans — in the hope of "a disturbance", she told Joe Holloway, the well-known diarist.

They were to be largely disappointed. The play, according to the *Irish Independent* the next day, "earned many hearty laughs, and was applauded by a packed house." Yet Joe Holloway in his diary records emphatically that "all words and no play makes *Faustus Kelly* a dull boy." The acting was good, with F. J. McCormick as Kelly, Cyril Cusack as the Town Clerk, and Liam Redmond as "The Stranger", but the play and its language did not come up to expectations. Patrick Kavanagh agreed with Holloway when they discussed it later, adding, "I hate all bloody vulgarity." Producers have since found that though the play starts well, the second and third acts fail badly. The words were all there — O'Nolan was never less than a talented wordsmith, and had been richly rewarded by his hours in the Dail — but there was no real dramatic structure or conflict.

Other reviews echoed Kavanagh's doubts about the vulgarity of the language. The play, which had been published in volume form at the same time, ran its allotted fortnight. O'Nolan claimed later that political pressure had been applied to suppress his sharp satire on Irish public life. But like so many of the legends he spread about himself and his work, this was not true.

This was not his only theatrical venture at this time. He had only just sent his play to the Abbey when he was approached by Hilton Edwards of the Gate Theatre. For a Christmas show at the Gate at the end of 1942 O'Nolan wrote a one-act play *Thirst*, which has since proved the most reliably entertaining of his plays. (It is included with *Faustus Kelly* in the posthumous volume, *Stories and Plays*.) The American critic Richard Watts, who was then working for the American government in Dublin, was more amused by Myles' play than by another piece in the same programme by Oscar Wilde. O'Nolan made drink more attractive than Wilde made lust, he commented.

He suggested to Hilton Edwards a play on "horrible concepts of time and life and death that would put plays like *Berkeley Square* into halfpenny place." Nothing came of this. But towards the end of July 1942 Edwards asked him to attempt an Irish version of the play *From the Insect World* by the Czech dramatist Karel Capek. O'Nolan based himself on the standard English translation, but set the play in St Stephen's Green, and gave the characters different kinds of Irish accents. The play was produced by the Gate Company and ran at the Gaiety Theatre from 22 March to 27 March 1943.

From the reviews it seems that the audience felt that O'Nolan had trivialised the thematic importance of the play, which it must be remembered is one of the classics of European theatre. It may have been O'Nolan's intention to continue his satire of Dublin life by other means. He localised the universal to make it accessible on his own terms. Capek's butterflies (beautiful and ineffective) became O'Nolan's wasps; his crickets were now chirping with Cork accents, and his beetles were born and bred on a Dublin dungheap.

Though his friend Brinsley MacNamara, the theatre critic in the *Irish Times*, thought the play lost none of its pungency as satire, a correspondent of the *Evening Mail* expressed

---

1942   2 (Crockett's)   FEBRUARY

19 THURSDAY

Six Weeks have passed. Scene is the living room of Mrs Ellen's house. The room is comfortable and furnished with taste but is evidently being used as the headquarters of an election campaign and is on that account somewhat awry. Pinned to the back wall are two disarranged posters. One reads VOTE FOR KELLY AND A NEW BROOM. The other NOT FOR PARTY OR PRIVILEGE BUT FOR COUNTRY AND PEOPLE — KELLY. There is a door LEFT and another RIGHT. On a side table are boxes of envelopes and stationary, a few brass musical instruments and a megaphone. In a corner stands an enormous furled tricolour.

21 SATURDAY

A bell)

P.T.O.

THIS IN SINGLE SPACING

22 SUNDAY

(The scene is the same save that the room is in a far more advanced state of disorder with electioneering posters, stationery, banners, flags and all manner of electioneering paraphernalia. A clock shows that it is about 9 in the evening. The curtains are drawn.

ELLEN is sitting disconsolately alone on the sofa, which is facing audience towards the left of the stage. KELLY is listening on the phone, bending over a small table towards the right. There is complete silence for a few seconds after the curtain goes up.)

KELLY: What? WHAT?

(Ellen sighs and passes her hand wearily across her brow).

KELLY (eagerly): Yes. Yes, yes! Good. good. Excellent. Yes? (he pauses to listen)

ABBEY THEATRE
— DUBLIN —

Proprietors · · · · The National Theatre Society, Ltd.
Directors · · · · Lennox Robinson, Richard Hayes,
Ernest Blythe, Roibeárd O'Faracháin
Managing Director · · · · Ernest Blythe
Secretary · · · · Eric Gorman

Monday 25th January 1943, and following nights
at 7.30

FIRST PRODUCTION OF

FAUSTUS KELLY
A Play in Three Acts by Myles na gCopaleen
Characters:

KELLY, Chairman of the Urban Council		F. J. McCormick
CULLEN	Members	Fred Johnson
REILLY	of the	Michael J. Dolan
SHAUN KILSHAUGHRAUN	Council	Brian O'Higgins
HOOP		Denis O'Dea
TOWN CLERK		Cyril Cusack
MRS. CROCKETT		Ria Mooney
HANNAH		Eileen Crowe
CAPT. SHAW		Gerard Healy
MR. STRANGE		Liam Redmond

ACT I.—The Council Chamber.
ACT II.—The living-room of Mrs. Crockett's house. Six weeks later.
ACT III.—The same as Act Two. A week later.

There will be Intervals of Ten Minutes between the Acts

Play Produced by FRANK DERMODY
Setting by MICHAEL CLARKE
Stage Manager—U. WRIGHT

ORCHESTRA
The Orchestra will perform the following selections :

Overture   Hungarian March   Berlioz (1803-1869)
IRISH AIRS :
(a) It is not the tear   arr. Dorothy Clifton
(b) Down by the Salley Gardens   arr. Herbert Hughes
(c) Suite of Airs   arr. Julia Gray
(d) The King's Cave   arr. Frederick May
(a) Two Songs—Wiegenlied and Feldeinsamkeit   } Brahms
(b) Excerpt—Trio in E Flat, Op. 40   } (1833-1897)

FADA Ó FUAIR MÉ FAOISEAMH

Fada ó fuair mé faoiseamh
Ó aislingeacha an tsaoghail
Ní h-iad a chéasas anois mé
Ach cuimhní géara na h-oidhche.
Ní innseochad fíos mo rúin,
Is leor a bhfuair mé de'n scorn,
Ní brúghfar go deo arís
Mianta na h-óige orm.
Ach chonnaic mé uaim an sliabh
A thógfainn le fonn,
Chonna-c mé uaim an bád
A sheolfainn anonn,
D'éirigh mé leis an sgatharnaigh
'S níor chreathnuigh roimh an lá,
A shamhailt ní dhéarna mé ariamh
Gur b'ionann tuile is trághadh.
Fada ó fuair mé faoiseamh
Ó aislingeacha an tsaoghail,
Agus cuimhní géara na h-oidhche
Imtheochaidh siad ar ball.

SEAMUS O'NEILL

ANNOUNCEMENT

DIA DOMHNAIGH 31/1/43 agus DIA LUAIN 1/2/43 ar 7.30 p.m.
Léiriú nua de
AN BHEAN CHRÓDHA
le Piaras Béaslaí

From the draft of Act II of *Faustus Kelly*
(opposite top).

From the draft of Act III of *Faustus Kelly*
(opposite bottom).

The programme of *Faustus Kelly*
(left).

the more general view that "the original framework was 'used' to 'put across' some rather banal topicalities more appropriate to the variety stage."

After that it would be some 22 years before O'Nolan was associated with another play in the Dublin theatre.

For all the coterie admiration of O'Nolan in Dublin, the enthusiasm of a foreign critic such as Richard Watts was more important. Watts, as guest critic in *The Bell*, wrote a long and appreciative article about Myles in the issue for March 1943. He also wrote about him in the New York *Herald Tribune* in April 1943. This in turn led to the article in the 23 August 1943 issue of *Time* magazine. Watts (so he later claimed) persuaded a small American publisher to import some copies of *At Swim-Two-Birds* into the country. But despite the enthusiasm of his fans, there was no success in sight yet for O'Nolan in America.

This was frustrating for O'Nolan, and after 1943, a change is readily detectable in his outlook. But this may also have been influenced by experiences in his professional life. Sean MacEntee was amused by O'Nolan. He was taken with the extraordinary skill with which he could, on the nearest hint, draft a letter expressing exactly what he wanted said. (His daughter the poet Maire MacEntee puts this down to O'Nolan's skilful parodying of her father's official style rather than any real insight.)

O'Nolan had impressed his superiors as a civil servant, at least until this date. MacEntee who enjoyed him as a kind of court jester, appreciated these other talents as now became evident.

On the night of 23 February 1943 a convent industrial school in the main street of Cavan town was burnt down. Some 32 children were killed. No nuns were injured. It was said that they had kept the doors locked because they did not want the firemen to see the young girls in their night clothes. But this evil rumour was merely a reflection of the incompetence which had led to the tragedy. The scene following the fire were sordid in the extreme. The charred fragments of the little broken bodies were shovelled into eight coffins and buried in a common grave. Why were the doors locked? How was it the nuns had escaped? The papers, especially the *Irish Times*, thought there were serious questions to be answered.

As Minister of Local Government Sean MacEntee appointed a tribunal to investigate the cause of the fire and to make recommendations. The chairman was Jack McCarthy S.C., assisted by Major Comerford of the Dublin Fire Service, and Mary Hackett, a Dublin social worker. The matter was a sensitive and controversial one, and in the delicate position of Secretary to the Tribunal, he appointed Brian O'Nolan.

The hearings began in Cavan town during the second week of April 1943, during which

Cavan Plunged In Woe

36 DEATHS IN FIRE AT ORPHANAGE

Desperate Rescue Efforts Made

("Irish Independent" Special Representative.)
Cavan, Wednesday.

"Take us out, take us out, we are suffocating."

THESE words, screamed by young children, still linger in the hearts and minds of the people of Cavan who, this morning, witnessed the terrible fire which completely destroyed one wing of the orphanage run by the Poor Clares in the main street, here.

Of the total of 85 inmates of the institution, 36—35 girl orphans and a aged cook —now lie dead as a result of the greatest holocaust this country has seen since the disaster in Drumcollogher in 1926.

The debris was still smoking when I arrived in the town, and firemen were still playing the hoses lest the fire should flare up again.

The fire was first seen by Miss Cissie O'Reilly, who, from her room, saw the flames leaping skywards. She raised the alarm, and Mr. Louis Blessing, the well-known Ulster and Cavan footballer, and Mr. John McNally came on the scene. ...

Mr. Blessing ran to inform the Guards, but when he had returned the fire had taken a firm hold.

It is believed that it originated in the laundry, situated beneath the dormitory, in which the children had been trapped.

RAGING INFERNO.

Terror-stricken children ran screaming from the building, which was a raging inferno in a matter of minutes. Some in their night clothes, dashed from the town into the fields.

From upper storeys children leaped down 40 feet to escape the devouring flames. Some were taken to the County Hospital with

Bishop of Kilmore (Most Rev. Dr. Lyons) visiting the Orphanage ruin.

The charred stairway down which ma attempted to escape.—*Irish Indepe*

The Orphanage ruin at Cavan.—*Irish Independent* Photo (H.)

News items on the day of the Cavan town fire 25 February 1943 (*above*).

Official government report on the orphanage fire, drafted by O'Nolan (*opposite*).

the convent was inspected several times. Later the tribunal sat for three days in Dublin. Their report was issued in September. It was bland in its conclusions, for in the Ireland of that day it would have been impossible to arraign an order of nuns, especially the Poor Clares who ran the Cavan convent. The question of compensation (which seems to have been raised in private by O'Nolan) was avoided in public. It was established that the fire had begun in the laundry, that no blame attached to any individual, but that more careful precautions should be taken in future.

The tribunal specially thanked O'Nolan for the care and consideration he had given to their needs. Indeed it is likely that much of the report was in fact originally drafted by him for the tribunal. (These were the "affairs of state" which so impressed the *Time* editor who interviewed him that summer.)

In private O'Nolan was less bland: one night sitting with T. F. O'Higgins (now Chief Justice) in a local pub he gave vent to his real feelings (as O'Higgins recently recalled):

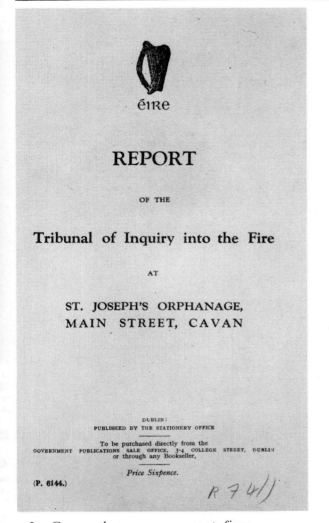

éɪʀe

REPORT

OF THE

Tribunal of Inquiry into the Fire

AT

ST. JOSEPH'S ORPHANAGE, MAIN STREET, CAVAN

DUBLIN:
PUBLISHED BY THE STATIONERY OFFICE

To be purchased directly from the
GOVERNMENT PUBLICATIONS SALE OFFICE, 3-4 COLLEGE STREET, DUBLIN
or through any Bookseller,

Price Sixpence.

(P. 6144.)

In Cavan there was a great fire;
Joe McCarthy came down to inquire.
If the nuns were to blame.
It would be a shame,
So it had to be caused by a wire.

In later years O'Nolan (as his wife recalls) would aver to the subject of the Cavan fire, and his memories of the event never faded. In its combination of indifference, pettiness and lack of charity, the disaster encapsulated much of what he felt was wrong in the Ireland of his day. The matters of state which O'Nolan had to deal with, revealed to him on a daily basis the true realities of Irish life. Was it any wonder he became a changed man in the later 'Forties.

Naturally much of his work as a government officer was merely routine. But in the course of time he grew sceptical about the whole matter of public service. Taking a friend down a corridor in the Customs House, he suddenly stepped sideways and threw open the office door on two startled clerks deep in the racing pages of the papers. "Look at them," he jeered and slammed the door.

One revealing document has escaped the net of secrets about his official work. It is an inter-office memo written by O'Nolan about the heads (that is the outline form) of the Superannuation Bill, which dealt with the pensions of local government officers. This was written in 1944; the bill itself was not passed until 1948.

The proposed legislation, according to O'Nolan, represented the "advanced social thinking" of 1944. It was at once repressive and paternalistic, tying the individual down on the one hand by not allowing him to make provision for his own pension, and on the other hand insisting on forty years of service before he was entitled to an official one. Future events in his own life make these bitter comments of 1944 read ironically.

His stance showed in what he wore. He was always dressed in a suit, waistcoat, long dark overcoat and wide-brimmed hat. This was the standard uniform of the civil servant. Indeed part of his advance from *At Swim-Two-Birds* had gone on buying a black hat. O'Nolan wore, basically, the same clothes for forty years. Towards the end of his time in the civil service some of his critics thought indeed that they were the same clothes, worn everyday of the year, a striped suit of an odd addled strawberry colour.

It is difficult to believe this was so. The verminous narrator of *At Swim-Two-Birds* had overlaid the legend of his creator. O'Nolan was never a bohemian, and resented any such imputation. John Ryan recalls that he attacked Patrick Kavanagh when he pointed out that Myles' tie was stained with mucus. To attack the man's appearance was a shorthand way of attacking the man himself.

O'Nolan never spoke with a Northern accent. He had a sharp, even petulant way of speaking, in a Dublin accent he had cultivated, what might be called a refined gurrier accent. (Gurrier is Dublin argot for an urchin, or any low type, as might be a punk or a Teddy Boy.) His ear had adapted itself long ago to the argot of the pubs he frequented. He preferred the tough bars and quayside pubs, such as Mulli-

HEADS OF SUPERANNUATION BILL
_____

[handwritten: Notes by Myles was Sheehan (Nolan)]

The present draft may be taken to contain a statement of the advanced
official thought of 1944 on human and social issues, such as are necessarily
involved in the idea of superannuation. Considered as such, the draft is
ominous. Part ll aims to give pensions to road-workers but will not permit
the few shillings concerned to emerge without gigantic bureaucratic
convulsions. The first provision in the process of giving the men pensions
is - characteristically - that they may get no pensions at all. Either they
are entitled to pensions or they are not; there is no justification for
providing that a man shall be conceded a vital right or denied it at the whim
of councillors. There is no apparent necessity for the monstrous
paraphernalia of applications, declarations, certificates, appeals, and
soforth. No road worker, unequipped with a university education, could be
expected to make his way through this jungle of legalistic mysticism on the
mere assistance of "a notice explanatory of the provisions thereof."

Part lll aims to give local officers the same 'rights' as those conceded
to civil servants and seems to proceed on the assumption that the civil servant
is heaven and that no sane person could conceivably wish for any dissimilar
paradise. This admiration on the part of civil servants for the civil
service system is most significant. The civil service superannuation code at
present in operation in this country is a semi-penal system devised in another
age by the British Treasury to ensure docility and progressive emasculation on
the part of its servants. It is unjust, cynical and immoral but achieves its
purpose so well that many of its dupes have come to regard it as a divinely
ordained norm; any pension system incompatible with it is bad but a system
conforming to it is not only good but represents the final fulfilment of all
legitimate human aspiration. Psychologists recognise that in conditions of
exceptional morbidity, the sufferer conceives his disorder to be a precious
possession and a great delight; he pities others who are not subject to it
and will consider that he is conferring an enormous favour by communicating it
to them.

The draft proposes to reinforce and perfect in relation to local officers
superannuation provisions similar to those in operation in the civil service.
In the civil service the entrant commences his career with a period of
'probation'. Actually he can be sacked at any time and is in fact on
probation throughout his official life. The formally prescribed period of
probation is his first official invitation to be timid and 'good'. This is
quite a small thing but it is interesting to observe with what unfailing piety
the same mean little provision was recently imparted into local appointments.

The entrant to the civil service from the outset suffers a cut of about
15% in his pay in respect of 'pension liability'. Such a deduction could be
defended only if itwere in the nature of an assurance premium, which would
guarantee the officer or his representatives in certain eventualities a
pension or lump sum which would not vary according to the number of premiums
paid or the time at which the contingencies provided against materialised.
This is what any prudent person would arrange himself if the State agreed to
let him manage his won private affairs and his salary. In fact he gets no
pension at all if he has to retire before he has served 10 years. If
inescapable personal circumstances compel him to quit the civil service after
?8 years service, he gets no pension at all. The entrant's first ambition
is to succeed in keeping his nose clean for 10 years. He is then
'pensionable' i.e., he cannot voluntarily leave the civil service without
suffering great financial loss. His next goal is retirement at the age of
65 or after 40 years service. He now knows he is in f or life and moreover
that the previous pension, rosily maturing over the years, can be wiped out by
a single serious lapse. He becomes a mouse.

/The

gan's of Poolbeg Street or the Scotch House on Burgh Quay, to the places frequented by the arty crowd.

In that era the Palace Bar in Fleet Street, where Smyllie held court, was the pre-eminent arty place. Cyril Connolly on a visit to Dublin at the end of 1941 was brought there by John Betjeman: he thought it "as warm and friendly as an alligator tank, its inhabitants, from a long process of mutual mastication, have a leathery look, and are as witty, hospitable, and kindly a group as can be found anywhere." Among the types he describes O'Nolan must surely be "the fuddled philosopher with a glass in front of him." Brian O'Nolan is featured in Alan Reeve's famous cartoon "Dublin Culture" which dates from this period. The artist Patrick O'Connor, one of the few survivors of those drawn by Reeve, recalls that in the early 1940's O'Nolan was never seen drunk. Indeed at first he did not even know he was a writer. Such was the atmosphere of the pub that few reputations went unscathed.

Little wonder O'Nolan preferred the Scotch House, on the corner of Hawkins Street and Burgh Quay, across the river from the Customs House. The Scotch House was frequented by congenial civil servants and by journalists from the *Irish Press*, people with whom he could keep silence or play chess. The association of Myles with the Scotch House was well-known enough for him to refer to it in the late Forties period of *Cruiskeen Lawn* as "My Office". When the pub was closed he wrote an elegiac piece on the auction which he attended with nostalgic regrets for his early days.

By 1944 as a man and an artist he was entering upon a new and difficult period of his life.

O'Nolan as uncivil servant: his notes on the heads of a new government bill (*opposite*).

Flann O'Brien recommends The Palace Bar to the serious drinker (*this page*).

The Uncivil Servant

If O'Nolan drank little enough in the early Forties, that had changed by the end of the decade. As a writer he had been active, indeed over active until 1943. Then a change took place. There are no more books (at least none by Flann O'Brien or Myles na Gopaleen), no more plays, and the tone of the column began to change, assuming a brutal harshness it seemed to many in Dublin.

After he returned from the fire tribunal in September 1943, he was moved from his previous post over to the Roads Section, as assistant principal. The move, on the face of it, does not look like a promotion. In 1948 he was made Principal of the Town Planning Section. There he was cut off completely from the daily activities of the government which he had relished as the Minister's Private Secretary. And though his new position has serious responsibilities, he does not seem to have cared much for them.

The Town Planning section in the late Forties and early Fifties was involved in many questions of planning in Dublin which presented the city corporation with a severe problem. The officials in the corporation felt that O'Nolan and his section were not playing their part. Some felt it quite improper that he should turn up drunk at meetings in the afternoons. He was, it seemed to one of them, quite simply bored.

For a person interested in power and influence, a senior rank in the civil service was an ideal base. But power did not interest O'Nolan. Influence yes, but only as he could exert it through his column. Certainly he seems to have been bored. It is to this period that many of the stories of the drunken Myles belong.

He would arrive in his office in the morning and, as had long been the case, do one and a half hours work, clearing his desk of files it took others all day to work through. By 11 o'clock he was over in the Scotch House. He would leave his hat and coat on the stand outside his office, so that his loyal secretary could tell any callers that his hat and coat were there and, therefore, he must be about the building somewhere. Bored with his work, he was also frustrated as a writer.

It was at this period, beginning in 1946, that he published the first set of Stephen Blakesley thrillers. Whatever fun there may have been in writing these, money must have been his motive, not now to support his family so much as to support his drinking habits. O'Nolan, in the opinion of a medical friend of his, James Deeney, was killing himself with Bass' No. 1 Barley Wine, a highly alcoholic brew, which turned his complexion a blackish hue.

"I'll give you a couple of months, if you don't follow my advice and give it up," he told him. O'Nolan turned on his friend, calling him a bloody Papist. But soon after, in one of those pyschologically motivated accidents, O'Nolan broke his leg and was laid up in hospital and at home for a few months, separated from all alcohol.

He needed to exert some control over his life. O'Nolan had always found a readier sympathy among the girls in the civil service than among his more off-hand male colleagues. In 1948 he proposed to one of the girls who worked in the typing pool at the Customs House, and who had often taken his dictation. Her name was Evelyn McDonnell.

Under the title 'Dublin Culture', this cartoon of the Palace Bar by the New Zealand caricaturist Alan Reeve was published in the *Irish Times* in 1940. The regulars were: BACK ROW (from left-hand corner): John P. Colbert (with pipe), G. H. Burrows, Francis MacManus (standing), Patrick Kavanagh (centre back), Brian O'Nolan, Liam Redmond, Donagh MacDonagh (standing), John Chichester (seated, right-hand corner), Austin Clarke, Padraic Fallon, F. R. Higgins. MIDDLE ROW (from left): (standing with camera) Alec Newman (seated at table below camera), Ewart Milne, Lynn Doyle, Leslie Yodaiken, Roibeard O Farachain, M. J. MacManus (in black hat),

(standing) Tom, one of the barmen. Centre table (from left) R. C. Ferguson, Esmonde Little, R. M. Smyllie, Brinsley MacNamara (below), William Conor (looking at book) Seamus O'Sullivan, Right hand table (at top) Cathal O'Shannon, Jerome Connor, David Sears (at bottom) George Leitch, Desmond Rushton. BOTTOM ROW (from left): Alan Reeve (black suit and beard), G. J. C. Tynan-O'Mahny, A. J. Leventhal, Edward Sheehy (Centre table front) Patrick O'Connor, Harry Kernoff, Sean O'Sullivan. Bottom (right) Jack, Sean and Mick, the barmen.

Inside the Palace Bar *(facing previous page).*

Myles at the bar, holding forth *(left)*.

The Brother (played by Eamonn Morrissey) toasts his creator *(opposite)*.

She says she was surprised when he asked her out, and even more surprised when he asked her to marry him. But she found him congenial, and enjoyed his humour. They were married on 2 December 1948 in Rathmines parish church.

They kept the wedding a secret. There were no guests, only their best man and bridesmaid as witnesses. The first his colleagues knew of the matter was when he went down to the accounts section and asked to be put on the married scale. When news of his marriage reached the Pearl Bar, to which the *Irish Times* people had now migrated, the alligators expressed their pity for the woman who would take on Myles na Gopaleen. She had no need of their pity, then or later.

Evelyn O'Nolan had no doubts about what she had done, whatever troubles the future held. She was devoted to him, as his old friend Niall Montgomery observed in an obituary, and he to her. In the stronghold of his private life, O'Nolan now had an ally against the wider world. He was going to need one.

At this date *Cruiskeen Lawn* was taking on a less fanciful turn. Myles had always been adept at avoiding libel actions, which is extraordinary given his material. There had been only one incident of the kind in the history of the column. In a piece in 1942 he had discussed the Institute of Higher Studies, a special project of de Valera's, on the staff on which were the Celtic scholar T. F. O'Rahilly and the refugee physicist Erwin Schroedinger. The first had recently suggested that there was some historical confusion over the identity of St Patrick, while the other had spoken of the material basis of life. It was too much for Myles. Higher studies should be a matter for private pursuit and should not be paid for out of public funds. The Institute in its short existence, Myles observed, had managed to prove that there were two St Patricks and no God.

The directorate of the Institute were furious and issued a writ against Myles and the *Irish Times*. The matter was settled out of court, with the paper agreeing to pay £100 damages.

CRUISKEEN LAWN

By MYLES NA gCOPALEEN

THERE was a play at the Abbey recently called "The Cursing Fields." I am sorry I missed it because I knew them well. As lads we were forbidden to have anything to do with the family or play with the Fields boys. The reason was that they all used appalling language. Often old Mrs. Fields used to come up the lane at dusk and curse in through the hedge at my parents. Sometimes old Fields himself would swear horribly at me through a window when I would be passing by on my way to school. Even the youngest of them, a stripling of ten, had a repertoire of curse-words that would surprise a sea-faring man. One of the older boys emigrated to the States and is now said to be a respectable and valued citizen there. A thing that I doubt very much.

* * *

The National Library could be defined as a place where books accumulate and man Dick Hayes; save that to make puns on personal names is recognised the world over as the mark of ill-breeding and a loutishness of intellect, not to say a bankruptcy of ideas.

·That nothing but the Best is good enough for the Institute of Advanced Studies is another quip that must, in the name of reticence and that delicacy of manner which distinguishes the gentleman, remain unsaid. Here, at any rate. By all means pass it off as your own in the boozer to-night. The laugh that you will get will be as forced and as false as your own claim to be a wit.

* * *

Talking of this notorious Institute (Lord, what would I give for a chair in it with me thousand good-lookin' pounds a year for doing "work" that most people regard as an interesting recreation), talking of it, anyway, a friend has drawn my attention to Professor O'Rahilly's recent address on "Paladius and Patrick." I understand also that Professor Schroedinger has been proving lately that you cannot establish a first cause. The first fruit of this Institute, therefore, has been an effort to show that there are two Saint Patricks and no God. The propagation of heresy and unbelief has nothing to do with polite learning, and unless we are careful this Institute of ours will make us the laughing stock of the world.

* * *

I was in a shop the other day and noticed a card, one of those cards the theatres send out, advertising cards in

fact. It said

Lord Longford presents
THE KINGDOM OF GOD
produced by Gerald Pringle.

Recently I read in the London *Times* a report of a company meeting addressed by Major the Rt. Hon. the Earl of Hardwicke. Referring to the company's staff, he said that "they were doing work of real national importance in helping to put before the public a line of wines, spirits and renowned cocktails which cast out depression, brace up resolution, banish fatigue and doubts . . ."

* * *

Flash ! Rushed yesterday to Dublin's red-brick non-sweepstaking Baggot-streethospital were Siamese twins, complaint being overstimulation of thairoid gland. Flash !

* * *

Pabulum supplied by certain cheap sensational Irish papers could be called Feis, Flash, and Good Red Herring.

The *Cruiskeen Lawn* article that led to the trouble with the Institute of Advance Studies *(left)*.

Erwin Schroedinger *(bottom)*.

Professor Alfred O'Rahilly *(opposite left)*.

Cartoon of Myles by Alan Warner, in which O'Rahilly, *Time* and others have their legs pulled, and the Scotch House features as the pagoda *(opposite right)*.

Only £50 was ever paid. What seemed the right thing to do in 1942, now embarrasses the Institute, who would prefer not to recall the matter.

The remark that led to that action was at least humorous. That cannot be said of what Myles was writing a decade later. By then he was becoming vindictive and more personal in his attacks. In 1951, arising out of the furore of the government medical scheme of Mothers and Children which brought down the first Inter-party government, a feud began with Alfred O'Rahilly, a brother of the aforementioned Celtic scholar, formerly of Blackrock College, then President of Cork University. This had nothing to do with the political row in the country at large. It was a clash of personalities, an exchange between equals, for O'Rahilly was able to give as good as he got. In previous exchanges he had worsted G.B. Shaw and Evelyn Waugh. Myles was as nothing to him, he was a "hired humourist" of the alien *Irish Times*. Myles was furious, and lashed back. But, the exchange showed him at his weakest.

The column did not appear for much of 1952, for O'Nolan was having one of his periodic tiffs with the editor. He was writing instead for *Kavanagh's Weekly*, a paper edited by the poet and his brother Peter, which was a *succès de scandale* for a brief season before the money ran out.

O'Nolan was also writing a third series of detective stories, again under the name

Stephen Blakesley. These seem to have been written on his office typewriter, for his wife has doubts about his authorship of them based on the fact that she never saw them at home. Here again he was writing for the money.

Eventually he returned to the column, beginning a new feud with Dublin Corporation, and with the Lord Mayor of Dublin, Senator Andy Clarkin. An Tostal, a tourist promoting scheme of the period was a special bugbear. This involved not merely various festive events, but the unveiling of a civic decoration in the middle of O'Connell Bridge,

which included as a centre piece a flame in red plastic, in the midst of a flower bed. Myles found the apposite title for this curious edifice: "The Tomb of the Unknown Gurrier," a Dublin riposte on the Tomb of the Unknown Soldier. But within weeks his ribaldry had encouraged a gang of engineering students to rip the flame from its foundations and throw it into the river Liffey. It was never restored. Only the flower bed, bereft of dignity, remained, a forlorn memorial to wounded civic pride.

The feud with Clarkin was a more extended affair. Myles had observed that the clock over his coal store in Pearse Street was always stopped. He ran in his column the cryptic acronym ACCISS — which stood for "Andy Clarkin's clock is still stopped." Those in the know realised it stood for Ask Ciss, the good man's wife, on whom he depended for social advice. Here the fun became too personal. No larger purpose was being served, except the humiliation of a self-made man. Evelyn warned him. Was he not going too far this time? He ignored her.

Clarkin himself seems to have enjoyed the affair, especially as a photograph of the clock being admired by Myles appeared in the *Irish Times*. Publicity never does any harm. But Myles now turned to more formidable targets, to Aer Lingus and to CIE. The local branches of Fianna Fail grew restless. Myles was known to admire their opponent in the Dail, James Dillon alone among politicians, and it always seemed to be Fianna Fail men who got the stick. The sharp political tone of the column was asking for trouble. Soon it came.

The inevitable happened. One evening in 1953 O'Nolan returned home to his house in Mount Merrion Avenue. "I've been fired," he announced baldly. Evelyn was shocked. Civil servants, as she well knew, could not be fired. "If you don't believe me, ring John Garvin then." She did. And it was true.

Of course, an official gloss was put on the matter. When O'Nolan had been promoted to Principal of Town Planning, he had refused to take the medical. (He simply would not have passed.) He was therefore in an acting capacity only in his post. Now he was to "retire" on medical grounds. The civil service doctor had ruled him unfit to work. Worse still, as Evelyn learnt, he was to have no pension.

From that horror they were at least saved by the intervention of John Garvin. O'Nolan got £4 a week. The dismissal of a civil servant is a serious matter, which ought to have received Cabinet consideration. As O'Nolan had officially "resigned" this may not have been the case. But it is worth recording, that having been patiently protected and tolerated by men like Sean McEntee, he was forced out while Mr Patrick Smith was Minister of Local Government.

Mr Smith had represented Cavan in the Dail since 1922. Did the ghosts of those unfortunate children in the Cavan convent fire hover in the background of Brian O'Nolan's resignation? This is a tenuous link perhaps, but the by-ways of Irish politics are strange and curious in the connections they make.

Fr Dineen, the lexicographer supreme of the Gaelic Revival (*above*).

"The Tomb of the Unknown Gurrier" — **the Tostal flame on O'Connell Bridge** (*opposite*).

John Garvin, who saved O'Nolan's pension *(top)*.

The Customs House *(bottom)*.

Through the Trough
of the Fifties

The disaster of O'Nolan's dismissal, which became effective in April, 1954, was more than enough to explain the condition of the man a few months later on the first Blooms-day, the scene on which this book opened.

Having lost his salary, it was essential that he find some new means of support. This he could best do, he thought, by extending his field of journalism. In December 1954 he sent a round robin letter to the editors of the provincial papers in Ireland, offering a column, of which a sample was enclosed, at a cost of 1 guinea an article. A column in Irish was available if there were enough subscribers.

The scheme was modelled on the syndicated columns that are such a feature of the American press. He hoped that the cachet of Myles na Gopaleen would encourage the editors. But there were few takers, despite his assurance that the material would be light, and non-controversial. Over the next decade or so his columns appeared in the *Longford Leader*, the *Southern Star* in Skibbereen, and the *Nationalist and Leinster Times* in Carlow. He also wrote columns for the Irish edition of the *Sunday Despatch*, and for the *Sunday Review* (a tabloid published by the *Irish Times*), as well as individual articles for Irish magazines and British papers.

Aside from this journalism, he also did a certain amount of odd-jobbing for friends in the printing trade, and advertisements for such things as Guinness and the Hospitals Trust Sweep stakes.

He also pursued any likely job that came along, all without success. When the Belfast station of Ulster Television opened in 1955 he offered them a play, *The Boy from Ballytearim* which had been inspired by the Mourne songs of the poet Moira O'Neill. It was not produced. Other schemes were mooted, for a musical, and later for an opera.

The figure that was seen constantly about the streets at this time was, in fact, working continuously. He lived at 81 Mount Merrion Avenue, and was a familiar sight making his way with marionette steps down to the Widow O'Rourke's, his favourite pub in Blackrock. He saw a great deal of John Ryan in those days.

An early memory is of him telling me how on one balmy July Sunday morning he found himself in the garden there with his dog and nothing to do, for it was the dreaded hour of 10 am and the pubs would not be open for another two and a half hours. He flung himself into a deck chair and groaned. 'I had a hangover,' he recalled, 'which would have hanged twenty full-grown men—and the little dog just sat in front of me, his eyes looking into my soul and like all dogs being a perfect reservoir of sympathy and understanding. At length he sprang to his paws and dashed into the lush undergrowth. From the frantic stirrings of the verdure I assumed that he was locked in combat with a rat. But no, he was dragging out an inanimate object, namely a bottle, and not an ordinary bottle but a bottle of Powers' Gold Label whiskey—full! You see we had a party the night before and some crafty gate-crasher, sensing that there might not be sufficient uisce-beatha to go around, had hid his contribution in the undergrowth, as a second line of defence, if the worst came to the worse! And then they will tell you that dogs don't think. Think is it? That dog of mine could argue Kant's Critique of Pure Reason with you if he could talk, which fortunately he can't.'

(O'Nolan was a confirmed dog man. The dog in the above extract was a fox terrier who died of old age in 1961. He then got a young Airedale which he called Hackett, after one of the characters in *The Dalkey Archive* on which

MAIRÉAD GILLAN

BRIAN Ó NUALLÁIN
do chuir i nGaeilge

BAILE ÁTHA CLIATH
OIFIG AN tSOLÁTHAIR

he was then working. The dog grew into "a giant George Bernard Shaw faced" guardian of its owner's doorstep in later years according to one wary visitor.)

When he was in the civil service, he had written all his *Cruiskeen Lawn* columns in one stint on the Sunday afternoon, sitting at the dining room table. Now he wrote them day by day, or rather night by night, on his return from town. John Ryan recalls taking O'Nolan home one evening the worse for wear, and typing out, to O'Nolan's dictation, the copy for delivery to the *Irish Times* the next day. O'Nolan sat in his chair, gazing into space, the sentences and paragraphs emerging fully

Brian O'Nolan at ease with his friend Brinsley MacNamara *(top)*.

The MacNamara play which O'Nolan translated into Irish *(bottom)*.

A demonic Myles, envisaged by Robert Ballagh *(opposite)*.

SLIEVENAMAN, MOURNE MOUNTAINS

The Mourne Mountains . . .

. . . and another side of Northern Ireland
(*top and bottom*).

A George Knowall article from the
***Carlow Nationalist* (20 June 1962).**

**James Joyce, increasingly a figure of fun
for O'Nolan** (*opposite left and right*).

THE NORTHERN IRONY

ISN'T IT INCREDIBLE? In this low-slung island, this Jem of the silver sea, this other Aden, this paradise girded with rocks, dusk, playboy fisherfolk in Youghals (and occasionally George Burrows) we have two Prime Ministers! Where is that vaunted economy one hears so much about from the politicians?

And the dear knows I believe both of them are from over the water. Think of history's backdrop, of O'Neill, the great Earl of Tyrone and ask yourself whether he will forgive me for saying it) the name of Mr. Terence O'Neill is not a bit ridiculous? And Lemass! So far as I can trace the line that was a group of Huguenots who arrived at Littlevmouth in the 16th century with little bags full of heads and a few broken tapestry looms. Both parties done all right for themselves, and I suppose we could call both landings the beginnings of the tourist trade.

One sees mention in the papers of a "dialogue" between Lemass and O'Neill about the abolition of what people insist on calling the Border. Why don't they look up a dictionary and find out what that word means? The preposterous thing should be called The Split (holy political word in the south) or The Schism (venerable ecclesiastical term). But there's a neat remedy for it:

If O'Neill won't stop troubling
Good statesmen in Dublin,
He should get a brush-off
In the manner of Khrushchev.

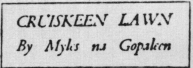

CRUISKEEN LAWN
By Myles na Gopaleen

MY LITTLE SCHEME is simplicity itself. Book a room in some pleasant, greasy back sittingroom in a hotel in Monaghan town. There by appointment will be met Lemass, myself, O'Neill, and some reputable party to make a fourth --James Dillon, Professor Desmond Williams, the Pope O'Mahony or Hilton Edwards. Pack of cards, of course, and a runner at the ready for the stout, malt and hang sangwiches. After initial courtesies, many hands of poker with simultaneous ingestion of tavernous mendicaments, a few songs and perhaps pious aspirations, the southerners will say something like this:

"Now look at here, O'Neill. We're all tired of this play-acting and your wee parliament at Stornaway. Harold Wilson thinks you're a damn nuisance and Douglas-Home never heard of you. If necessary we'll look for the plantation of Scotland. But meantime, if you don't come into our garden and play with us, we'll give ye Partition so exhausting that ye'll think it's Parturition. *We'll build a Wall!*"

And we would mean it: each county responsible for its own portion of the Wall, with generous grants from the Dail under a

Monster Employment Scheme. Walls are an ingredient in Irish history; you had the walls of Limerick and Derry walls. Now we would have what even Dubliners would have to call the North Wall, the very negation of movement and mercantile traffic.

* * *

WELL OF COURSE there would be difficulties—nothing more certain if architects were allowed in on the job. The houses in awesome Fitzwilliam street were all put up by a journeyman plasterer, with no nonsense about trigonometry or "quantities." Architects would talk of the "curtilage" of the Wall, its "environ," the necessity for "light," the importance of "access," architraves, pediments and all that gear. The Wall should be absolute, with watchtowers at intervals of a mile for guards with searchlights armed with elephant guns. There would not be a door even for the G.N. train and do you know (ah, vain hope!) the Wall might be *permanent!*

The funny G.A.A. inexplicably regard handball and chess as native Irish games, though failing to ban the incontrovertibly alien diversions known as tennis, golf, croquet, squash. The Wall would surely greatly encourage handball, and Protestant deviationists might even try to import the Eton wall-game. Wall-eye? I wouldn't be afraid of that affliction, nor of any smugglers' cant about Ireland's Wall-street. To the Barricade!

From Clongowes to Martello tower

WELL, boys-ah-dear, there was the queer hosting at the Forty-Foot swimming hole, Sandycove, Dun Laoire, when a great number of people—perhaps 200—gathered to honour James Joyce.

His great book *Ulysses* is very long (my own edition is in two volumes) but its events are confined to a single day and night, namely, June 16, 1904; and its opening is located on the top of the Martello Tower at Sandycove where Joyce himself, Oliver St. John Gogarty and an Englishman were in residence.

Ceremony?

On display in the tower itself were various relics of the master, including letters, printers proofs and his death-mask, the last-mentioned an extremely successful cast, ironically a thing in death that was extremely life-like.

The location of Saturday's ceremony (if drinking small ones and cups of tea can be called a ceremony) afforded a curious historical conspectus. Those towers are an echo of the Napoleonic wars when the British with three ships of the line and two frigates sought with artillery to subdue a tower commanding the Gulf of San Fiorenzo.

It was only through a sheer accident—the igniting of junk on the tower which should not have been there at all—that it was eventually taken. Then it was found that the tower had only two 18-pounder guns, the military lesson was obvious and was quickly learned by the British. The fear of the French invasion of the home territory was immediately provided against by the wholesale erection of the so-called Martello towers around the whole coast of England and along the eastern shores of Ireland. They are so solid and massive as to be virtually indestructible and many centuries hence will no doubt rank with our round towers as objects of speculation and wonder.

The Clongowes Boy

The wonder of Saturday's event was that it happened at all. Even ten years ago it would have been unthinkable but in more recent years the austerity and beauty of Joyce's work is finding acceptance in quarters where it had formerly won condemnation without any investigation of its worth. Even as an historical portrait not only of Dublin but of an age *Ulysses* is unique.

Joyce had left a full picture of his early self in his *Portrait of the Artist As A Young Man*, one of the finest autobiographies in the English language. To a large extent however all his writing concerns himself, his life and times. Many chance acquaintances, including people who wished him ill, have been immortalised.

Having at last shed the silly mantle of purveyor of erotica, Joyce emerges from contemporary accounts of him as a very shy man, punctilious in manner and very formal in modes of address. Sylvia Beach, an American in Paris who had the courage to publish *Ulysses*

originally in 1922 and who was present on Saturday at Sandycove, an alert lady of 75, was never known or referred to by Joyce otherwise than Miss Beach.

Joyce went to school at Belvedere College and Clongowes, both institutions run by the Jesuit Fathers, and left Ireland for good at the age of 22. Left it physically, that is. His mind

GEORGE KNOWALL

and memory never left Dublin. He died in 1941, during the war. Would it not be an idea to disinter the remains and rebury him at his own beloved city?

James Joyce was born on February 2, 1882, at Rathgar and from Clongowes went to University College, Dublin, where he specialised in modern languages. He went to Paris in 1904 and for the rest of his life lived variously in France, Italy and Switzerland.

His last work, *Finnegans Wake*, is accepted as one of the most complicated and obscure pieces of writing ever to see print and if there is substance in the common belief that great mental stress and worry lead to ulcers, it is understandable that his death arose following collapse from duodenal ulcers amid the chaos of the German occupation of France.

Friends at this time urgently counselled him to go to the Irish Minister in Paris and get his British passport changed for an Irish one, for it was known that the German authorities regarded him as a British spy. He refused, saying "it would not be honourable."

Owed Nothing

That was another manifestation of his stiffness and formality. He certainly owed the British nothing, for they were the first to burn *Ulysses*: of 500 copies landed at Folkestone in January, 1923, the customs authorities seized 499.

T. S. Eliot has remarked that Joyce was the greatest master of the English language since Milton. Let us leave it at that.

fashioned. Ryan was astonished. It was as if there was a file of ready-made columns in his mind, which needed only to be drawn on at will.

After leaving his article in the office, O'Nolan would pass the day in a tour of the pubs, going from, say, Sinnott's, to Neary's, and on through MacDaid's, Doheny and Nesbitt's, Mulligan's, wherever his fancy roamed. There were occasional bashes, when he resorted to the pubs around the Cattle Market as already mentioned or to some hotel where a discreet knock would obtain a drink after hours. But generally he was on his way home, not sober perhaps, but early enough by four o'clock.

This drinking must be kept in proportion, for it went hand in hand with a vast amount of weekly work. This is not the feat of an alcoholic, as a comparison with Brendan Behan suggests. Behan had ceased to work by the end, even to dictate. O'Nolan remained in control.

At this time O'Nolan and Behan were friends of a kind. Miss Mae O'Flaherty, of

Parson's Bookshop on Baggot Street Bridge, a famous resort of many famous literary figures, recalls Behan blowing in one morning with a small, dark man in tow. Having conducted his business in his usually flamboyant manner, Behan and his friend departed. A moment later Behan slipped back into the shop. "Did you know who that was?" he asked. No, said Miss O'Flaherty.

"That was Myles na Gopaleen."

"Who would have thought it," said Miss O'Flaherty, "he seemed so insignificant."

"That's the point," said Behan, and blew out again.

Later Miss O'Flaherty became more familiar with the figure of Brian O'Nolan. He would slip into the shop, and hover like a shadow among the shelves of books. He used the set of the Oxford Dictionary which she had supposedly for sale as a reference book, extracting the hard facts with which to belabour government ministers. A Minister of Agriculture (probably his old enemy Patrick Smith) had suggested that the cream head on the pint should be siphoned off and used to feed animals. Myles, on consulting the dictionary, discovered that it was nearly all air. Nothing could be fed on it. This typically inane ministerial notion was duly roasted in the column.

That was the real O'Nolan, insignificant in the corner of the bar, with his glass in front of him, book or paper in hand. If you did not know who he was you might not have noticed him. He must have felt that he had been reduced to a mere hack, that the important projects of which he talked would come to nothing. The end of the 1950's found him in danger of declining into that doomed frustration which had engulfed so many of Dublin's writers.

His college friends all seemed to have prospered. Niall Sheridan for instance had had stories published in international publications such as *Atlantic Monthly* and *Esquire*. Donagh MacDonagh had a play published by Penguin Books. Mervyn Wall had also had a great success with his satirical *Fursey* novels.

Only Patrick Kavanagh seemed to share O'Nolan's backwater. Patrick Kavanagh had been involved in February 1954 in suing a paper which he said had libelled him, but he had been torn to shreds in the witness box by J. A. Costello, the former Prime Minister now returned to being a barrister. Soon after this O'Nolan and Kavanagh were invited to the L and H to discuss the topic of Irish newspapers, one as victim, the other as a master of attack.

"It was with a combination of curiosity and confidence that the proceedings would be far from dull that the students flocked to the meeting," Michael O Riain recalls. "They were not disappointed. The guests strongly disapproved of one another's remarks, to the great amusement of the audience, and those present will long remember Liam McCollum's welcome to the guests, delivered from a bench in the middle of the theatre, because the

Brendan Behan, whom O'Nolan admired in many ways *(opposite)*. **Patrick Kavanagh, an important figure in O'Nolan's set** *(above)*.

crowds were too great to permit his descent to the rostrum.''

This smacks of a Roman circus, in which two wild beasts would be set upon each other for the delight of the comfortable citizens. The indignity of the spectacle was compounded by the fact that at that date neither the work of Kavanagh nor that of O'Nolan had received any respect or recognition. Perceived as clowns, they could respond only with snarls. As artists they had no other form of protection.

But this period was to bring further shocks. After his father's death, his mother had stayed on in Avoca Terrace, which remained the family home, the centre of the children's lives. When Brian married, he chose to live nearby, and was on hand for such things as Christmas dinner. However in the early 1950's Agnes Nolan's health declined, and the house became too much for her. She gave it up and went to live with one of her daughters. In 1956 Mrs Nolan died.

Brian refused a trip to Russia with Anthony Cronin and James Plunkett for fear of being far away when her end came. He was deeply affected by her death. He asked his brother Kevin helplessly how it was that "We ———s deserved or came to have the mother we had." There was no answer to that.

The night his mother died O'Nolan was in McDaid's pub with John Ryan, and Patrick Kavanagh (with whom he was then at odds) came up to sympathise with him.

"Yes," said Kavanagh, "there is only one real death in your life and that's your mother's."

The tears trailed down O'Nolan's face. He could say nothing. He hoped for a time to find a way of writing about his mother. But he failed. Then at last he did so, but as always in the oblique and distanced manner he found for dealing with the feelings that meant most to him.

Writing an appreciation in *Cruiskeen Lawn*

''Pots and Pains'' — the domestic side of Myles — an imaginary scene *(top).*

O'Nolan's house in Merrion Avenue where he lived in the early 1950s *(bottom).*

Agnes Nolan as her son Brian liked to recall her *(opposite)*

The exterior of the Palace Bar . . .

. . . and Mulligan's of Poolbeg Street, both used by Myles *(opposite top and bottom)*.

The comedian Jimmy O'Dea, in the part of Biddy Mulligan *(top)*.

Neary's in Chatham Street, used by actors and writers *(bottom)*.

some months later, of Thomas O Crohan's book about the Blasket Islands, he chose to translate from the original Irish a short passage dealing with the death of the author's mother:

The weather remained fine until I reached my mother in her native retreat of Ventry—a long way from the Great Blasket, between sea and land, and although there was a good funeral turnout, plenty of carts and horses, it was on people's shoulders that she went to the graveyard.

That was the end of the two who put the sound of this language into my ears the first day. May God's blessing be on them.

"Most of us have to mourn the death of parents," O'Nolan concluded, "But surely to call them 'the two' is the utmost in legitimate pathos."

After his mother's death, O'Nolan and his wife moved to 10 Belmont Avenue, in Donnybrook, an address much nearer the centre of town.

The editors of a history of the L and H asked him to contribute an account of his own experiences in the society during his college years. This memoir is interesting in that it was one of the very few pieces of personal writing that he did not make fanciful. It reminded him of his youth and of the "brilliant" reputation he had once had in UCD. In the General Election of 1957 he decided he would stand for one of the Senate seats representing the National University, following the example of his friend Professor W.B. Stanford, who had represented Trinity since 1948. It was a paid job and he would be able to speak his mind with ease in the second chamber of parliament. He would be able to take part in public affairs, instead of just commenting on them.

According to Patrick Kavanagh O'Nolan took his chances of election very seriously. He expected to top the poll. On election day he reproduced in his column a letter address to Senator Myles na Gopaleen, Santry Great Hall, which had been redirected to the Senate

The funeral scene from *A Hard Life*, drawn by Patrick Swift (bottom).

O'Nolan in a publicity picture of the 1960s (opposite).

Myles on a rural journalistic assign- **Myles by Harry Kernoff, the picture that**
ment with Patrick Gallagher — the **so angered O'Nolan** *(opposite page).*
article was never written *(above).*

by the post office.

The Senate election was held on 9 May 1957. There were three seats open. The valid poll was 9,515, which meant that under the proportional system used in Ireland, any candidate needed 2,379 votes to be elected. O'Nolan came bottom of the poll with 389 votes and was eliminated on the first count.

There was no reference to this defeat in his column. Even for Myles na Gopaleen some things were better passed over in silence. His supporters numbered little more than the 244 people who had bought *At Swim-Two-Birds* in 1939. It was a terrible reminder of the true dimensions of an Irish writer's real following. His life seemed now at its lowest ebb. Perhaps it was time for the tide to flood in again.

**Myles, the Man and the Masks, painting
by Robert Ballagh**

A Reputation Recycled

Sometime in 1958 or early 1959, O'Nolan approached the writer Sean O'Faolain, then the Director of the Arts Council, with a curious request. He gave O'Faolain the typescript of *The Third Policeman* and asked him to give him his opinion of it. As such modernist literature was not much to O'Faolain's taste, and as he planned to resign his post shortly in any case, he handed the book on to Mervyn Wall, the Secretary of the Arts Council.

Mervyn Wall had long been familiar with the legend of this lost book, having heard all about it from Donagh MacDonagh in the 1940's. He began to read it with great interest, but before he had got very far, O'Nolan arrived at his office demanding its return. He was not pleased with it as it stood, despite Wall's enthusiasm for what he had read. O'Nolan, he gathered, planned to make another book out of what seemed to him to be the best parts of it. Neither O'Faolain or Wall can now be certain of the exact date of this incident.

During the preceding years, Evelyn O'Nolan had asked her husband about the book. He had told her too that it was not right: that he planned to recast it from the first person to the third person. Was this the germ of his later novel *The Dalkey Archive*, in which bicycles and policemen also play a large part? Whatever the truth of that, it is clear that O'Nolan was hoping to be able to make some use of the only complete book which he had to hand. Whatever these plans were, they were suddenly dropped.

In May 1959 he received a letter from a young publisher in London named Timothy O'Keefe, who then worked for MacGibbon and Kee. He had long been an admirer of *At Swim-Two-Birds*. If it could be arranged, his firm were now prepared to reissue the book.

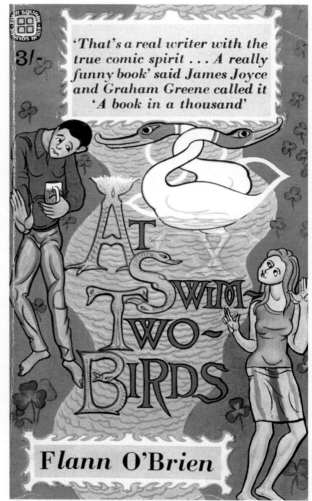

'*That's a real writer with the true comic spirit . . . A really funny book*' said James Joyce and Graham Greene called it '*A book in a thousand*'

The delightful jacket of the first mass-market edition of O'Nolan's masterpiece

O'Nolan sent him the original contract from 1939. Soon Longmans' interest had been surrendered and plans were advanced for the novel to be republished the following year.

O'Nolan at this stage considered the novel

Poster for an Abbey Theatre adaptation of *The Hard Life* in 1985 *(opposite)*.

Scenes from *The Hard Life:* walking on air . . .

. . . the brothers in the bar . . .

. . . and Mr Collopy and friends reach the Vatican, illustrations by Patrick Swift *(this page)*.

O'Nolan in the 1960s, drawn again by Sean O'Sullivan *(above).*

O'Nolan in the autumn of 1960, soon after the release of his novel *(opposite page).*

Pleading with the Pope, the climax of the stage adaptation of *The Hard Life* *(following page).*

quite dead. The American publication in 1951 had fallen flat, and he had made gifts to his friends of copies that remained from that edition with scornful comments. That it had a new chance was wonderful.

The effect of this on O'Nolan was extraordinary. Now it was no longer a matter of touting for influential opinions to get *The Third Policeman*, a rejected book, published, but a matter of a forgotten but much-praised book at last getting the reception it deserved. This appeared in July 1960 to a uniformly rapturous welcome. It was reissued in a paperback, in an American edition, and in several translations.

Inevitably many reviewers, seeking some kind of parallel in the past, mentioned James Joyce. By now Joyce was no longer the influential figure admired by O'Nolan in the 1930s. Joyce's skill with dialogue and his

humour, those were things he could still admire. But the Joyce of academic scholarship, which concentrated on matters of structure or myth, was not congenial to him, or to many other Dubliners of the day.

Yet Joyce could not be so easily dismissed. By the time the novel was launched in August 1960 he was at work on another book, *The Hard Life*. This title had been mentioned in *Cruiskeen Lawn* a few years before, but that is no indication that he wrote any of it at that time. The book draws heavily on the Dublin of James Joyce, taking its cue from Mr Bloom's musings on the lack of ladies' toilet facilities in the city of Dublin in *Ulysses*. The spur to write it may have been the publication in 1958 of Stanislaus Joyce's memoir *My Brother's Keeper* — which O'Nolan seriously considered to be a literary fraud. In a letter to Niall Montgomery he referred to *The Hard Life* as

"my dirty book". It must be said that O'Nolan's idea of what constituted a dirty book in
this era was sadly limited.

He called the novel "an exegesis of
squalor", and it returns to what Joyce once
called, in connection with his own work, "the
odour of ashpits." The Joycean overtones are
so obvious and so strong, that it should not be
overlooked that the book is set in an area of
Dublin in which O'Nolan spent some years of
his own childhood along with an elder brother
whose head was filled with great schemes.

Less obvious perhaps are the more personal
sources on which he may have drawn. Mr
Collopy, rendered on the dust jacket by his old
friend Sean O'Sullivan, was based on the
person of his former master in the civil service,
Sean MacEntee. The dialogues with Fr Kurt
Fahrt, S.J., the Jesuit who lived in the "House
of Writers", 35 Lower Leeson Street, are
taken to be a satire on the Society of Jesus. His
wife asked him once why he chose the Jesuits.
O'Nolan paused, and then said, "Because they
can take it." Indeed they could. O'Nolan's
funeral was to be attended by the Professor of
Maths-Physics at UCD, the Rev. Dr E.
Ingram, S.J., who lived like Fr Fahrt at 35
Lower Leeson Street.

This book then, like *At Swim-Two-Birds*,
contains jokes and references of so personal a
kind that they would be quite meaningless to
the ordinary reader, however well he knew
Dublin. But for O'Nolan these references
seem to have been an essential way of structur-
ing his material. He believed that *The Hard
Life* was "a very important book and very
funny. Its apparently pedestrian style is delu-
sive." The passages dealing with sexual disease, surely a key part of the book, are the
work of a man for whom some functions of the
human body could only be regarded with
disgust. Joyce may have provided the setting,
but the treatment owes a lot to Swift.

These books brought him in much needed
money. He and his wife had moved from
Donnybrook to a small bungalow in Stillorgan. It was bought in Evelyn's name. A will he
made in October 1962 during a serious illness
left his estate to her. His anxieties about
money did not abate. He complained to John
Jordan that he had an important book in him,
but he was mortgaged to the hilt. The tax
authorities were soon pursuing him, for he had
earned too much money in one or two years,
and much of it went in tax. When he drove a
car, he had regarded the police with great

O'Nolan's house in Belmont Avenue, Donnybrook *(opposite top)*.

O'Nolan's last home in Stillorgan *(opposite bottom)*.

Page from the manuscript of *The Dalkey Archive* *(this page)*.

From the typescript of *The Dalkey Archive* *(following page)*.

The date of departure of the last tram to Dalkey from Dublin may be crucial to the history of *The Dalkey Archive* *(following page)*.

suspicion. The tax men now replaced the police in his paranoid view as representatives of the oppressive state.

He still pursued jobs. Aside from literary projects such as a long book on Ireland or a history of the whiskey industry (a topic on which he could well claim to be a leading authority), he read for a Dublin publisher. He investigated positions as an administrative assistant, a translator in the Dail, and even a Junior Lectureship in Trinity College. He applied for the post of records officer when they did not want him as a lecturer. No job materialised.

In the view of those offering the jobs, O'Nolan was a hopeless case. It is not without a certain bitter irony that the first academic study of O'Nolan was written by a Trinity don, a decade after he had applied to teach there.

But, as a writer, O'Nolan was now at his peak. He had stopped writing in the *Irish Times* in 1962, but was enticed back a year later. The column was not as fresh as it had once been for him. The paper was now run by younger journalists, who had a new set of "Holy cows", he complained, and his copy was always being rejected or cut. The journalists on the other hand found that his copy was often slack and needed to be "knocked into shape" to make up the articles.

Television proved a more congenial em-

Dalkey.   Co. Dublin.

ployer. The BBC broadcast *Thirst* in 1960, Granada expressed an interest in *Faustus Kelly* and a version of *The Hard Life*, and his old friend Hilton Edwards, in charge of drama for the Irish television service, produced several of his plays. In February 1963 he was signed to write a series of fifteen 26 minute plays starring the Irish comedian Jimmy O'Dea. Called *The Ideas of O'Dea*, it ran from September 1963 through March 1964, achieving the highest ratings of all, making it a valuable property for the company.

The main work of this period was, however, another novel *The Dalkey Archive*, begun in September 1962. The original scheme was a brilliant one. In the course of his reading, he had concluded that St Augustine and St Ignatius Loyala, the founder of the Jesuits, had similar personalities. Both were reformed rakes, for instance, and both made much of their personal experiences of God. He did not care for either of them. He planned that the novel should include St Augustine, and that Loyala should be represented by that arch Jesuit, James Joyce.

By March 1963 the first 10,000 words had been written. O'Keefe was disappointed by the material he saw, but O'Nolan told him not to worry. The novel would eventually come together.

Brian O'Nolan painted by his brother, a portrait that now hangs in the Abbey Theatre with those of Yeats and O'Casey (*previous page*).

James Joyce about the age O'Nolan draws him in his novel (*opposite top*).

St Augustine in the medieval imagination (*opposite bottom*).

O'Nolan with his sister on a last visit to cousins in Strabane (*top*).

The Brian O'Nolan housing estate in Strabane, a curious memorial to the writer (*bottom*).

**De Selby's Theory, painting by Robert
Ballagh**

Some leaves from the author's salad days

I'm Telling you no Lie!

LIR O'CONNOR

I STARTED OFF IN life with somewhat of a handicap. Only those who were born in Ballyjoesullivan will know what I mean. The kindly caress of a mother's hand was denied to me from the beginning, as poor Mum had come to a tragic end some two years before I was born, having been fatally shot through the corsage in a saloon brawl. Someone had spoken lightly of a horse-jobber's name. Poor Dad was worse than useless at this time, having one foot in the grave, and the other, for nine months out of the twelve, confined within the narrow framework of a Thomas's splint. I often wonder how I ever managed to survive, but there—let us commence at the beginning.

The ragged storm clouds were veiling the face of the moon on the 3rd of September, 1886. Midnight chimed from the village church, and the sound of the bells had scarcely been whipped away by the fingers of the gale when, high above the soughing of the wind, there was heard the wailing cry of a new-born baby. For, that day and hour was I born, much to my uncle's and aunt's embarrassment. It is scarcely necessary to add that I was born with a caul, since practically every writer worth slandering was born with a caul, from Dickens down to Shelly. (I don't mean Percy B. Shelley, but a man named Fonsie Shelly I used to know who did odd pars for the old *Freeman's Journal.*)

Ah! If I had a mind to tell it, the subsequent history of that little caul would fill a good-sized book in itself. I could relate how, tied up with an old boot lace into a compact sphere, it helped me to win by a comfortable

---

A CHARACTER *I Could Never Forget. No. 30 of a series.*

LOOKING *back across the years of a lifetime as colourful as it has been exciting, I think I shall experience little difficulty in the selection of a suitable subject for this feature. For, I ask you, what more memorable, more breath-taking character could I possibly find to write about than my own inimitable self? True, in a volume of this size I can only hope to give the merest outline of a personality so vital that it might well have been the invention of some master of the romantic novel; but then this will be more than compensated for by the fact that my publishers will not be faced with the costs of the customary libel action which nowadays normally follows on every reference in print to any name, proper or otherwise, that is not, strictly speaking, one's own.*

—LIR O'CONNOR.

---

margin the senior hardball championships at Ballymun at an age when most boys are playing with their bead frames. Years later, when wintering in Siberia, it occupied the centre of the stage again. Most of my companions had died of cold and starvation. The very last pair of Russian boots had been ravenously devoured by us after having been converted into the savoury borsch that only the Russians can make. Day after day I could see the red-rimmed eyes of the others straying hungrily to the palatable tit-bit that I was using as a droshky rug. Let me cut a long story short by saying that it was only by sleeping with a half-cocked moose gun under my pillow at night

---

Article by O'Nolan under yet another of his pen names — how much more work of this kind remains to be found is a mystery *(above).*

There is though something mysterious about the origins of *The Dalkey Archive*. Some of the material is clearly derived from O'Nolan's recent reading of *The Third Policeman*, especially the theories about people turning into bicycles, and bicycles turning into people. Other parts seem to date from the 1940s. Anthony Cronin has observed that the trams which are referred to in the novel date it to the 1940's, as would the oddly old fashioned relations between the two boys and Mary in the novel's subplot. In fact the last tram to Dalkey ran on 10 July 1949.

More pertinent, perhaps, is the actual age of Joyce in *The Dalkey Archive*. He is clearly about 65 which would suggest that the year is about 1947. If the joke about him living secretly in a sea-side town outside Dublin was to have any impact, it must have been conceived when Joyce's last years were unknown, the only available biography coming to an end in 1939. O'Nolan was doing what he had so often done in the past, refitting an old piece of work.

Having this material to hand, O'Nolan could claim on the one hand to have begun the book (as he did in a letter to his American editor), and on the other admit (as he did to Tim O'Keefe a little later) that he had not yet done any writing. In making up *The Dalkey Archive* O'Nolan borrowed for the purposes of the plot, Niall Sheridan's home, which stood on the bluff overlooking the Vico Road in Dalkey. O'Nolan knew the area well as his solicitor, an old personal friend, also lived there.

The book also had for him a serious religious overtone. "There is, for instance, no intention to jeer at God or religion," he wrote to Tim O'Keefe, "the idea is to roast the people who seriously do so, and also to chide the Church in certain of its aspects. I seem to be wholly at one with Vatican II."

O'Nolan now seemed to be opening up more to the world, letting his guard down a little.

In March 1964 he published an article in an Ulster magazine *New Ireland*, edited by students at Queen's University, Belfast. He must have felt some fellow feeling for the student editor, for he promised him "sensational disclosures" about himself. These did not relate to his charmingly evoked memories of his childhood in Strabane — he had just been back there on a visit. They related to his own work. But such was his reputation as a joker that no-one took him seriously. He wrote:

In twenty-five years I have written ten books (that is substantial opera) under four quite irreconcilable pen-names and on subjects absolutely unrelated. Five of these could be described as works of the imagination, one of world social comment, two on scientific subjects, one of literary exploration and conjecture, one in Irish and one play (which was produced by the Abbey Theatre).

All this beside a mass of mere journalism.

O'Nolan believed seriously in the value of pen-names for protecting the integrity of the writer. But such a taste for false names does not make life easy for either the police or biographers. What are these books?

His novels, the play *Faustus Kelly* and *An Beal Bocht* can be accounted for in this list. But what are the others? They are clearly not the Stephen Blakesley thrillers mentioned earlier or his other pulp thrillers for the Sexton Blake Library, but much more serious and substantial works. Perhaps some are even under a female pen-name.

There is it would seem the exciting possibility that five major books by Brian O'Nolan remain as yet unidentified. Nor is it clear what unexplored nooks of his life they fit into. Brian O'Nolan is accepted as an important writer, but as yet the true dimensions of his literary achievement remain largely unknown.

Was this just another joke? Or was it a "sensational disclosure" as promised by a diffident writer who already sensed his end was near and did not want to die without making such a startling confession, leaving at least one sign post to areas of his life he had for too long protected.

De Selby and his whiskey, scene from Hugh Leonard's play *The Saints Go Cycling In* (opposite).

The Final Furlong

The Dalkey Archive was published at the end of September 1964. It was received with great enthusiasm —"the best comic fantasy since *Tristram Shandy*" according to one critic. Of all his books it was the author's favourite, a preference shared by many of his readers. It now seemed that Brian O'Nolan had got into his stride, and that there was the delectable promise of a new Flann O'Brien novel, not every second decade, but every second year.

Whatever he wrote would be read with interest. He had earned the right to experiment, even to fail. By now he was at work on a new novel, the working title of which varied, *Slattery's Sago Saga* being his final choice. Taking up the enthusiasm generated in Ireland

The young heroes from the stage adaption of *The Dalkey Archive* (*this page*).

Poster for the Gate Theatre production of the play in Cork (*opposite*).

Inside the Colza Hotel with Joyce, Fr Cobble and De Selby (*following pages*).

Underwater with Saint Augustine (*following pages*).

for John F. Kennedy and his family, it was to deal, in a Mylesian way, with the theme of the Irish-American. This was not a new O'Nolan theme: part of *The Children of Destiny* as he and his friends had projected it in 1935, had included the election of the first Irish American Catholic President. The novel was never to be finished. His American editor had serious doubts about the novel, which O'Nolan brushed aside. But here again, as was the case with all his books, revision would have turned what looks like dross into gold.

In the autumn Hugh Leonard wrote asking O'Nolan if he could adapt *The Dalkey Archive* for the stage, Dalkey being very much Hugh Leonard's piece of Ireland. His original plays had proved to be among the most popular of recent years, and his adaptions, particularly of Joyce, had earned him an international reputation.

O'Nolan was delighted, and gave him a free hand. He was also pleasantly surprised at the speed with which Hugh Leonard worked. "You undoubtedly have a thing I used to have—a prodigious capacity for hard sustained work," he said. The play was completed by June 1965 and was accepted for production under the title of *The Saints Go Cycling In*.

All did not go well with this relationship, however, for O'Nolan was accidentally sent a typing bill for scripts by Leonard's agent, and responded with brisk abuse.

Nevertheless O'Nolan could not help but admire how the playwright had handled the novel, even to providing a most effective final curtain. The frustrated dramatist in O'Nolan had found a success at last, and there was much he might have carried away from the collaboration, into his own work.

A second series of plays for Irish television, *Th'Oul Lad of Kilsalaher* with the well-known comedian Danny Cummins as the difficult old countryman attended to by his young niece, was in production. The scripts which O'Nolan provided had to be doctored by a skilled scriptwriter to make them more workable. The words, all the familiar Mylesian touches, were there, but O'Nolan still seemed to be defeated by the demands of dramatic structure. The 14 parts in 15 minute segments, ran from September to December 1965.

By then, however, something more ominous was needing O'Nolan's attention. Over the years he had been unfortunate in the number of accidents he had been involved in, breaking arms and legs more often than not. He had now broken his leg again. Meeting him casually Anthony Cronin asked about the leg.

"Did you ever hear of the dominant theme in a symphony?" O'Nolan asked. "Well, the leg is no longer the dominant theme."

For about a year he had been suffering from a continuous but diversified pain along the left side of his face. In March 1965 he consulted a specialist. O'Nolan had thought it was an inner ear affliction. The specialist said it was neuralgia, which O'Nolan eccentrically regarded as a "quasi-fictionious disease." A slight knotti-

OPERA HOUSE CORK

GATE THEATRE

presents

Hugh Leonard's

·THE SAINTS GO CYCLING IN·

Based on **THE DALKEY ARCHIVE** BY FLANN O'BRIEN (MYLES NA GOPALEEN)

from **Tues. 10th APR. 1984**
NIGHTLY **8.00 pm** ONE WEEK ONLY
BOOKING **(021) 20022**

WITH
Jim Bartley
Christopher Casson
Martin Dempsey
Aiden Grennell
Maire Hastings
Des Keogh
Garrett Keogh
Mary McEvoy
Barry McGovern
Johnny Murphy

DIRECTOR
Patrick Laffan
DESIGNER
Alpho O'Reilly

COSTUMES
Nigel Boyd
LIGHTING
Albert Cassells

Photo: Fergus Bourke/Design: Terry Monaghan

ness in the side of his neck led him back to his doctor. He was operated on, in the Mater Hospital. The pathologist who examined the removed tissue found evidence of secondary cancer.

He was sent for deep ray treatment at St Anne's Hospital in Northbrook Road. This treatment proved very disagreeable, and O'Nolan was racked by vomiting. He bore all of this with stoical courage.

Hugh Leonard's adaptation of his novel opened during the Dublin Theatre Festival at the Gate Theatre on 27 September, 1965. O'Nolan attended the first night, though he was clearly very ill. In a curtain speech he attributed his bodily ailments to St Augustine, who was wreaking his revenge for the mockery of him in *The Dalkey Archive*. Ever since he began that book he had been haunted by illness. He confessed that the only thing that cleared him up was a glass of strong whiskey.

In the foyer Hugh Leonard introduced O'Nolan to James Mason. "Ah, yes," O'Nolan observed, "I always admired you as an actor, long before you became a film star bollix."

The play had a long and profitable run, on into November. John Ryan asked him whether it would be transferring to London, the acid test, by Dublin standards, of real success. "Of course it will go to London, why the hell wouldn't it go to London." In that event, Ryan mused, some of his friends must arrange to go over. "A few of us? We'll charter a whole bloody plane! There must be enough sport-kings left in Dublin to fill a plane."

"Sport-king", with the meaning of a "piss-artist" or one of "the real lads", was an echo of the city slang of O'Nolan's youth, an echo even of uncle Joe Gormley.

The play never transferred. The plane never left.

The part of Sergeant Fottrell, created by Martin Dempsey, was a highlight of the Gate production. O'Nolan now suggested to RTE a new series of short television plays built around the character, again to be played by Martin Dempsey, called *The Detectional Fastidiosities of Sergeant Fottrell*.

In March 1966 he was still in correspondence with the television company about the series. But illness prevented him from doing little more than outlining the idea and the draft of an episode. He hoped to give the sergeant's station a timeless quality, and to allow him to range over wide areas with his musings. But as he explained in a letter to the controller of the station: "I am still very far from the land but one feature—vomiting several times every day—seems to have eased up."

After the opening of the play O'Nolan had had to enter St Luke's Hospital in Rathgar, where part of his treatment now included blood transfusions. It is difficult to know if he knew how ill he was. He knew he had cancer, but he had decided to go on as usual for as long as possible, even though that much abused body which harboured his multiple personalities was finally crumbling.

For the *Manchester Guardian* he wrote an article, "The Saint and I", which was published on 19 January 1966. He described his ideas about St Augustine, and how he suspected that the saint was the source of all he was suffering. Then with a casual calmness which must be admired, he admitted he had cancer.

So far a primary cancer has not come to light elsewhere in the body, but deep X-ray irradiation of the area caused a painful swelling, and there is evidence of generalised anaemia. Just now a visit to London for other advice and perhaps surgery is contemplated. I have not been in my health since I wrote that book or thought of writing it. I thank only Augustine.

This was written from bed. It was in St Luke's that Hugh Leonard and Phyllis Ryan (the producer of his play) visited him. They had brought a bottle of Paddy, the famous Cork whiskey.

He eyed the Paddy and at once rang a bell which summoned a little nun. "Sister," Myles told her solemnly, "I have two friends who are constipated and need a dose. Would you bring two glasses?" The little nun giggled, disappeared and returned with two tumblers for Phyllis and me. Between us we drank the Paddy and at last became friends for that last short afternoon. A few weeks later he was dead.

Dublin rumour spoke of O'Nolan's illness as "alcoholic poisoning", a claim which one still sees in print. In fact he had cancer of the pharynx, the soft tissue at the back of the palate, for which his lifelong smoking habit may well have been the cause. In the last two weeks of March the disease metastasised, spreading rapidly to other parts of his system,

generating itself. He lost touch with reality. He died suddenly on 1 April 1966 — April Fool's Day.

As the news spread among his friends, some thought it must be a Mylesian joke. They soon realised it was not.

The tributes were fulsome from all his friends; the finest, Evelyn thought, being one by Niall Montgomery (Kerrigan in *At Swim-Two-Birds*), who described his friend of over thirty years as "an Aristophanic sorcerer", but also recalled "the true compassion of a shy man" recalling a letter in Irish sent to a friend grieving for a sister's dead child.

The funeral, on 4 April, was a large one, from Kilmacud Church. John Ryan was astonished at the number of priests and nuns who attended, for he had never thought of Myles as a particular favourite of the clergy. There were even a number of distinguished Jesuits, an irony O'Nolan would have richly enjoyed. Nor had his old school forgotten him. There were no politicians.

At the graveside the rosary was recited in Irish, but there was no oration. This seemed strange to Ryan and Cronin as they came away. Yes, they agreed, someone should have said something.

The sergeant makes his entrance complete with bicycle (*previous page above*).

From Audrey Welsh's Abbey Theatre adaptation of *At Swim-Two-Birds* in 1981 (*previous page bottom*).

One of the last photographs taken of O'Nolan, already very ill (*top left*).

Evelyn O'Nolan, in 1985 attending the opening of the Flann O'Brien Symposium (*top right*).

The burial of Mr Collopy, drawing by Patrick Swift (*opposite*).

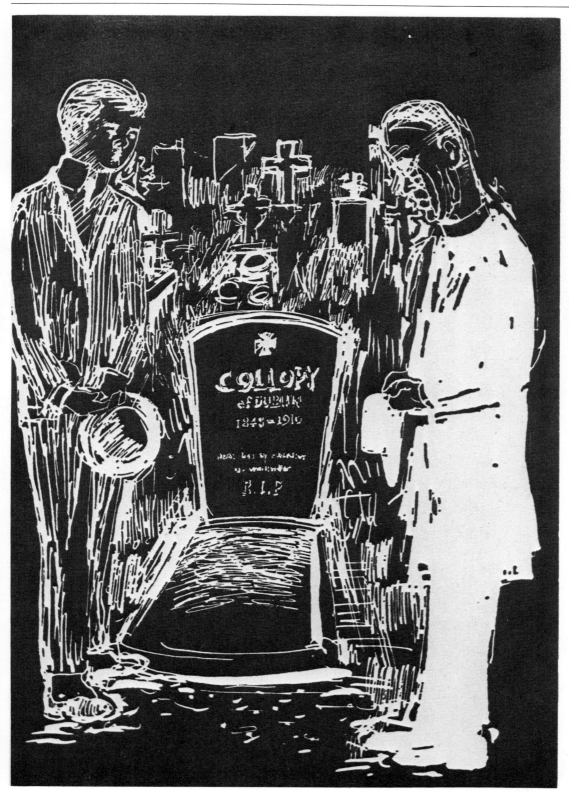

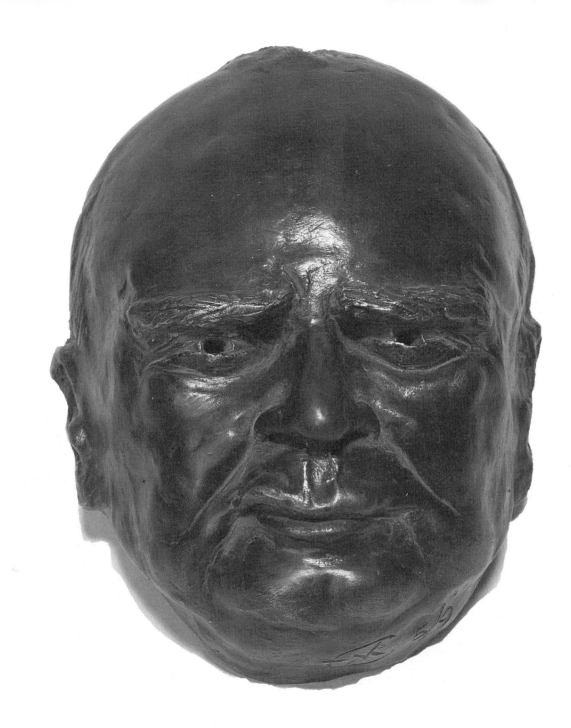

Mask of Myles made by Victor McCaughan *(above)*.

The eternal mystery: which is the third policeman? *(opposite)*.

EPILOGUE
The Return of the Third Policeman

The final joke was yet to come. Timothy O'Keefe was anxious to bring out whatever works of O'Nolan remained unpublished. A collection of *Cruiskeen Lawn* columns, a collection of plays and stories, and a translation of *An Beal Bocht*, all of which O'Nolan had resisted while he was alive, were now to be put in hand. But for immediate publication Evelyn O'Nolan sent him the typescript of *The Third Policeman*, which was published in September 1967.

It proved to be "a surprise from the grave", to borrow the phrase of Anthony Burgess. The great lost novel had at last seen the light of day. The book became, and remains, for a large number of his admirers, Flann O'Brien's masterpiece. The novel revealed at last the dark and alarming concerns of Brian O'Nolan's imagination. What had seemed unacceptable in 1940, now became a classic work.

Brian O'Nolan had the last laugh.

FURTHER READING

The various works of Brian O'Nolan, under his own name and as Flann O'Brien and Myles na Gopaleen:
At Swim-Two-Birds (London, 1939; New York, 1951; London, 1960; New York, 1961).
An Beal Bocht (Dublin, 1941; 1964).
Faustus Kelly (Dublin, 1943).
Cruiskeen Lawn (Dublin, 1943).
Mairéad Gillan (Dublin, 1953).
The Hard Life (London, 1961; New York, 1962).
The Dalkey Archive (London, 1964; New York, 1965).
The Third Policeman (London, 1967; New York, 1967).
The Best of Myles, ed. Kevin O'Nolan (London, 1968; New York, 1968).
The Poor Mouth, trans. Patrick Power (London, 1973; New York, 1974).
Stories and Plays (London, 1973; New York, 1976).
The Various Lives of Keats and Chapman and The Brother, ed. Benedict Kiely (London, 1976).
Further Cuttings from Cruiskeen Lawn, ed. Kevin O'Nolan (London, 1976).
The Hair of the Dogma, ed. Kevin O'Nolan (London, 1977).
A Flann O'Brien Reader, ed. Stephen Jones (New York, 1978).
Myles from Dublin, ed. Martin Green (London, 1985).

There is also a great deal of as yet uncollected journalism, under these and other names such as Lir O'Connor, as well as disputable works such as the Stephen Blakesley novels.

Brian O'Nolan's writings have been the subject of much critical discussion, but as yet there has been little published about his life.

The list below contains most of the items which will repay further reading by those interested in following up appreciations of his work or the intricate ways of his life.

The only full length critical work on Flann O'Brien is Anne Clissman, *Flann O'Brien: an introduction to his writings* (Dublin, 1975). This contains a short preliminary biographical chapter, based largely on the O'Nolan papers now in the University of Southern Illinois at Carbondale. **A new and revised edition of this book is in preparation.**

A good sampling of critical notions about O'Nolan can be found in the essays and articles edited by Ruediger Imhof, *Alive Alive O! Flann O'Brien's At Swim-Two-Birds* (Dublin, 1985).

A special number of the *Journal of Irish Literature,* vol. 3, no. 1, 1974, is devoted to Flann O'Brien and contains letters and other writings not available elsewhere including *The Insect Play.*

One of the most valuable investigations of O'Nolan's writings is Brendan O Conaire's *Myles na Gaeilge* (Dublin, 1986), written in Irish and dealing with the whole of his career in so far as it relates to work in that language. It is exceptionally detailed and all admirers of O'Nolan will find it of interest.

Brian O'Nolan wrote a short personal account of himself for *Modern World Writers* (New York, 1968), but was otherwise guarded in his biographical revelations.

His early life and family background have been described by his brother Ciaran O Nuallain in *Oige an Dearthar* (Dublin, 1973), a valuable book of which there ought to be an English translation.

Accounts of the man from several personal viewpoints (by Kevin O'Nolan, Niall Sheridan, John Garvin, Jack White and J.C.C. Mays) are to be found in *Myles* (London, 1972), a memorial volume edited by his publisher Timothy O'Keefe. The book also has a useful bibliography.

Other items of biographical importance are as follows:

Anon: "Eire's columnist", *Time*, 23 August 1943, p.90.

Arnold, Mavis: *Children of the Poor Clares* (Belfast, 1984).

Cronin, Anthony: *Dead as Doornails* (Dublin, 1976).

Hogan, Thomas (i.e. Thomas Woods): 'Myles na Gopaleen", *The Bell*, vol. 13, no. 2, 1943, pp. 129-140.

Jude the Obscure: "The H.U. Business Section", *The Honest Ulsterman,* July-August 1971, p.31.

Kelly, Seamus: "The Full of the Cruiskeen", *Irish Times,* 1 April 1976, p.10.

Meenan, James (ed.): *A Centenary History of the Literary and Historical Debating Society of University College, Dublin, 1855-1955* (Tralee, 1957).

Phelan, Michael: "Watcher in the Wings; a lingering look at Myles na Gopaleen", *Administration* (Dublin), vol, 24, Spring 1976, pp. 96-106. On O'Nolan as a Civil Servant.

Ryan, John: *Remembering How We Stood.* Second edition (Mullingar, 1987).

Wain, John: "To write for my own race," *Encounter,* July 1967, pp. 71-95.

White, Jack: "Rembering Myles", *Irish Times,* 1 April 1976, p.10.

Williamson, Bruce: "Man with an envelope", *Irish Times,* 1 April 1976, p.10.

ACKNOWLEDGEMENTS

This book derives from an exhibition mounted in Newman House, Dublin, for the Flann O'Brien Symposium in 1986. That exhibition was supported by University College Dublin, Cantrell and Cochrane and Guinness Peat Aviation, and we would like to thank Prof. Augustine Martin and the college authorities, Mr Brian Walsh, and Mr Brian McLoghlin for their interest in the project.

In writing this book we have drawn upon special materials in the Brian O'Nolan collections at the Harry Ransom Humanities Research Center of the University of Texas at Austin, and at the Morris Library, University of Southern Illinois at Carbondale, and we would like to thank those institutions for the generous assistance which they gave us.

We are grateful to Mrs Evelyn O'Nolan for her collections of many aspects of her husband's life and work. We would also like to thank Kevin O'Nolan, Miceal O Nuallain and other members of the O'Nolan family for the loan of pictures, photographs and books, and for sharing with us their recollections of their brother. Many friends and associates of Brian O'Nolan also helped us, some of whom have asked to remain unamed. John Ryan was of exceptional help to us at all stages.

Among those individuals and intstitutions who helped us we would like to thank: Dr James Deeney, Patrick O'Connor, Michael Lord Killanin, Sean O'Faolain, Mervyn Wall, Cyril Cusack, Niall Sheridan, Dr J. B. Lyons, Aileen Kelly, Patrick Gallagher, Barbara and Pat Pierce, Patrick Delaney, Noreen Kearney, Kevin Nowlan, Charles Aliaga Kelly, John Jordan, Ralph Steadman, Gus MacAmhlaigh, John Wyse Jackson, Anne Clune, Tess Hurson, Allen Figgis, Frank Litton, Victoria Cremin, Alf McLochlainn, Declan Kiberd, Brendan O Conaire, Mrs Sheila Iremonger, Dr John McCormack, Fr Sean Farragher, Peter Walsh, Margaret Costello, Mary Costello, Victor McCaughan, The *Irish Times*, The Northern Arts Council, The Institute for Advanced Studies,

Guinness PLC, The Library UCD, The Department of Folklore UCD, the National Library of Ireland, the Abbey Theatre, the Gate Theatre, the Irish Academic Press, RTE, the Garda Press Office, the Central Catholic Library, the Goethe Institute, Sachs Hotel, the Palace Bar, the Manuscripts Department, TCD, Fergus Bourke.

p.4: photo *Irish Times*
p.8: photo Tom Kennedy
p.14: photo *Irish Press*
p.16: *Irish Times,* 16 June 1954
p.24: painting by Pavel Tchelitchev, National Gallery of Ireland
p.24: bt, Patricia Hutchins papers, Manuscripts Department, TCD.
p.26: photos courtesy O'Nolan family
p.27: photos courtesy O'Nolan family
p.29: photos courtesy O'Nolan family
p.31: photos courtesy Miceal O Nuallain
p.32: tp, photo courtesy Kevin O'Nolan; bt, photo Joe Sterling
p.33: tp, Blackrock College Archives, photo courtesy Sean Farragher
p.33: bt, photo courtesy Kevin O'Nolan
p.35: Records Office, UCD
p.36: tp and bt, Peter Costello
p.37: Eason Collection, National Library of Ireland
p.38: tp, Peter Costello; bt, courtesy Brendan O Conaire
p.39: photo Neville Johnston, courtesy RTE
p.40: courtesy Brendan O Conaire; bt, photo Neville Johnston, courtesy RTE
p.41: photo courtesy Evelyn O'Nolan
p.42: tp, Records Office, UCD; bt, courtesy Liam de Paor
p.43: photo National Library of Ireland
p.44: Rheinisches Bildarchiv, courtesy Köln University; bt, Peter Costello
p.45: Peter Costello
p.46: Popperfoto, London; rt, courtesy Kevin O'Nolan
p.47: both Popperfoto, London
p.48: courtesy *Time* magazine
p.49: Popperfoto, London
p.50: Peter van de Kamp
p.51: Peter van de Kamp
p.52: both Records Office, UCD
p.54: tp, Peter Costello; bt, courtesy Chatto and Windus

p.55: courtesy Brendan O Conaire; lt, photo National Library of Ireland

p.56: Peter Costello; bt, courtesy Fr Francis Litton

p.57: tp, Records Office, UCD; bt, photo Neville Johnston, courtesy RTE

p.58-59: photo courtesy Harry Ransom Humanities Research Center, University of Texas at Austin

p.60: both courtesy O'Nolan family

p.61: photo Joe Sterling

p.62: painting by Miceal O Nuallain, courtesy of the artist.

p.63: photo National Library of Ireland; bt, Peter Costello

p.64: Holloway diaries, National Library of Ireland

p.65: photo courtesy Harry Ransom Humanities Research Center, University of Texas at Austin

p.66: courtesy of Alf MacLochlainn

p.67: Peter Costello

p.68: bt, photo courtesy Tom Garvin; rt, Lensman, Dublin.

p.69: tp, Peter Costello; bt, photo courtesy John McCormack, TCD.

p.70: tp, Peter Costello; bt, photo *Irish Times*.

p.71: courtesy Liam Miller

p.72: lt, Peter Costello; rt, courtesy Evelyn O'Nolan

p.73: tp, courtesy Declin Kiberd; bt Peter Costello

p.74-75: map drawn by Sean O'Sullivan

p.76: both Ralph Steadman, courtesy of the artist

p.77: both photos courtesy Department of Irish Folklore, UCD

p.78: tp, Ralph Steadman, courtesy of the artist; bt, both courtesy Brendan O Conaire

p.79: photo courtesy Department of Irish Folklore, UCD

p.80: tp lt, bt lt, courtesy Dr J. B. Lyons; tp rt, Harry Ransom Humanities Research Center, University of Texas at Austin

p.81: *Irish Digest*, April 1942, courtesy Central Catholic Library

p.82: both Harry Ransom Humanities Research Center, University of Texas at Austin

p.83: courtesy Alf MacLochlainn
p.84: photo National Library of Ireland
p.85: photo National Library of Ireland
p.86: Manuscripts Department, National Library of Ireland
p.87: Holloway diaries, National Library of Ireland
p.88: photo Joe Sterling
p.90-91: courtesy John Ryan
p.92: Harry Trumbore, courtesy Viking Penguin
p.93: photo Fergus Bourke
p.94: tp, *Irish Times,* bt, photo Pfaundler, courtesy Institute of Advanced Studies.
p.95: rt, photo courtesy Fr J. Gaughan; rt, courtesy Lord Killanin
p.96: Peter Costello
p.97: photo *Irish Times,* courtesy Frederick O'Dwyer
p.98: photo courtesy Tom Garvin; bt, photo Paul Kavanagh, courtesy Glen Photography
p.100: tp, courtesy Evelyn O'Nolan; bt, Peter Costello
p.101: painting by Robert Ballagh, courtesy of the artist
p.102: lt, *Irish Housewife,* 1963; rt, *Irish Times*
p.103: tp, National Library of Ireland; bt, drawing by Wyndham Lewis, National Gallery of Ireland
p.104: painting by John Ryan, courtesy of the artist
p.105: courtesy John Ryan
p.106: tp, Peter Costello; bt, photo Joe Sterling
p.107: photo courtesy O'Nolan family
p.108: photo Joe Sterling
p.109: painting by Harry Kernoff, courtesy Sachs Hotel; lt, photo Joe Sterling
p.110: drawing by Patrick Swift, from *Das Harte Leben*
p.111: photo *Irish Times*
p.131: photo Fergus Bourke
p.132: photo Fergus Bourke
p.133: courtesy of Gate Theatre
p.134-135: photo Fergus Bourke
p.136-137: photo Fergus Bourke
p.139: tp, both Fergus Bourke
p.140: both *Irish Times*

p.141: drawings by Patrick Swift, courtesy Goethe Institute, Dublin

p.142: bronze mask by Victor McCaughan, courtesy of the artist

p.143: Garda Siochana Archives, courtesy Garda Press Office

pp. 144-145: photo Fergus Bourke

Credit pages sequence: all Neville Johnston, courtesy RTE

pp.17-19: all courtesy John Ryan

p.21: photo *Irish Times;* bt, courtesy John Ryan

p.22: stills courtesy John Ryan

p.23: photo courtesy John Ryan

p.112: courtesy Patrick Gallagher

p.113: painting by Harry Kernoff, courtesy Sachs Hotel, Dublin

p.114: painting by Robert Ballagh, courtesy of the artist

p.115: courtesy Four Square Books

p.116: courtesy Abbey Theatre

p.117: drawings by Patrick Swift, courtesy Goethe Institute, Dublin

p.118: drawing by Sean O'Sullivan, courtesy Mrs. Evelyn O'Nolan

p.119: Lensman, Dublin

p.120-121: photo Fergus Bourke

p.122: photos Joe Sterling

p.123-124: Harry Ransom Humanities Research Center, University of Texas at Austin

p.124: bt, Peter Costello

p.125: painting by Miceal O Nuallain, courtesy Abbey Theatre

p.126: tp, Peter Costello; bt, Mary Costello

p.127: tp, courtesy O'Nolan family; bt, Strabane District Council

p.128: painting by Robert Ballagh, courtesy of the artist.

p.130: Central Catholic Library

A NOTE ON THE AUTHORS

Peter Costello is a literary historian and biographer, living in Dublin, who has written books on the Irish Revival, James Joyce and Jules Verne. He was educated in Dublin and is a graduate of the University of Michigan.

Peter van de Kamp, who has a PhD from University College Dublin, where he taught for some time, now teaches in the English Department of the University of Leiden in his native Holland. He is an authority on the poetry of W.B. Yeats, and is working on a biography of Katherine Tynan.